Medieval Exegesis in Translation

Commentaries on the Book of Ruth

Commentary Series

General Editor

E. Ann Matter, University of Pennsylvania

Advisory Board

Seth L. Brody, Haverford College
John C. Cavadini, University of Notre Dame
James J. O'Donnell, University of Pennsylvania
Thomas H. Seiler, Western Michigan University
Lesley J. Smith, Oxford University
Grover A. Zinn. Oberlin College

The Commentary Series is designed for classroom use. Its goal is to make available to teachers and students useful examples of the vast tradition of medieval commentary on sacred Scripture. The series will include English translations of works written in a number of medieval languages and from various centuries and religious traditions. The series focuses on treatises which have relevance to many fields of Medieval Studies, including theories of allegory and literature, history of art, music and spirituality, and political thought. The translations strive for clear, straightforward English prose style. Notes are meant to provide sources and to gloss difficult passages rather than to give an exhaustive scholarly commentary on the treatise. The editions include short introductions which set the context and suggest the importance of each work.

Medieval Exegesis in Translation

Commentaries on the Book of Ruth

Translated with an Introduction and Notes

by

Lesley Smith

Published for TEAMS
(The Consortium for the Teaching of the Middle Ages, Inc.)

by

Medieval Institute Publications

WESTERN MICHIGAN UNIVERSITY

Kalamazoo, Michigan — 1996

Second Printing 2006

Library of Congress Cataloging-in-Publication Data

Medieval exegesis in translation : commentaries on the book of Ruth /
    translated, with an introduction and notes, by Lesley Smith.
        p. cm. -- (Commentary series)
    Includes bibliographical references.
    ISBN 1-879288-68-0 (pbk.)
    1. Bible. O.T. Ruth--Commentaries--Early works to 1800.
2. Bible. O.T. Ruth--Criticism, interpretation, etc.--History-
-Middle Ages, 600-1500. I. Smith, Lesley (Lesley Janette)
II. Series.
BS1315.M43 1996
222'.3507'0902--dc20   96-29069
                                        CIP

ISBN 1-879288-68-0

Printed in the United States of America

Cover design by Linda K. Judy

Contents

Acknowledgements

One of the pleasures of scholarship is the opportunity it provides for working with others, especially in an area requiring wide general knowledge. I am most grateful to Martin Kauffmann, Philip Krey, Ann Matter, Michael Signer, Sr. Benedicta Ward, SLG, Mary Sheldon-Williams, and Joseph Ziegler for sharing their expertise so graciously.

Introduction

The Book of Ruth

This book brings together and translates from the medieval Latin a series of commentaries on the biblical book of Ruth, with the intention of introducing readers to medieval exegesis or biblical interpretation. The Bible was the ubiquitous book of the Middle Ages. Its influence pervaded all aspects of medieval life, yet study of medieval biblical commentary is neglected. There are a number of reasons for this, having little to do with the importance of biblically derived ideas in medieval life. Most of the material is in Latin, the language of educated discourse from the Roman Empire to the Reformation; much is unpublished, existing only in manuscript, often in abbreviated or note form; and the exegesis assumes a wide background knowledge of references and allusions which very easily pass us by. Medieval scholarly methods are subtle, relying on the elegant variation on the conventional point rather than the easily spotted difference. All of this makes the field a difficult one for beginners to enter: a small sample of exegesis taken out of context may be incomprehensible or misleading. The purpose of this book, then (and indeed, of the series), is to act as a useful gateway for the student considering the study of exegesis as a field, as well as to stand as a study of the commentaries themselves.

Ruth is the shortest book of the Old Testament, being only four chapters long. It is partly for this reason that it lends itself so well to a short book introducing medieval exegesis; but it is also of interest in itself. Ruth poses a number of exegetical problems, including the basic one of why such an odd book, in which God never appears as an actor, and with a central character who was *not* an Israelite but a Moabite outsider, and a woman at

that, should find a place in the canon of Scripture. For Jewish readers, Ruth is an example of God moving in mysterious ways and using unlikely human material: the point of the story is the genealogical table at the end of the book—Ruth is the great-grandmother of David, greatest of the kings of Israel. This explanation also held true for Christian readers, since Jesus was born into the "house of David," but their exegesis added a typological dimension. For them, the story of Ruth was one long allegory, with Ruth appearing in the character of the Church, Boaz as Christ, Naomi as that part of the Synagogue, or of the Jews, who become the early Church, and Orpha as the unrepentant Synagogue, which did not turn to Christ. Ruth becomes the bride of Boaz as the Church becomes the bride of Christ; she clings to Naomi, her roots, while walking onward into Boaz's embrace. Orpha returns to her native land, as the Synagogue Jews refused to leave their old religion.

Modern scholars date the writing of the book between 950–700 B.C., and probably earlier in that spread rather than later. They regard it as a fiction set in history, since the historical details of the book are accurate, though there is no evidence for the specific events narrated. Ruth is a book of great charm and narrative craft. Much happens in the short space, and the original Hebrew composition is subtle and powerfully done, with great control of the language. For example, the text plays beautifully on the contrasting themes of emptiness and fullness. In the first chapter, Naomi tells the women that the Lord sent her away full, with husband and sons, and has brought her back empty, a childless widow. In chapter two, when she has gleaned in Boaz's field, Ruth takes back to Naomi barley and the remains of her evening meal, "so that she was made full." After the encounter on the threshing floor, in chapter three, Boaz gives Ruth six measures of grain so that she would not return to Naomi "empty." In the last chapter, Boaz (and God) makes Ruth "full" by fathering a child—a child who also fills up the emptiness of Naomi's womb, from chapter 1. Finally, the theme overarches the whole story, for the Israelites begin the tale empty, in exile to escape from the famine in their own land, with no sense of future, and end it back in their own land, with the fullness of the hope of the great King David to come.

The original language of Ruth is sometimes unusual and the syntax difficult. Those places where the translation may seem particularly stilted or strange probably reflect the difficulties of a Latin which, in turn, reflects the difficulties of the Hebrew. These difficulties remain for modern Hebrew translators and were not a function of medieval ignorance.

Ruth is described by Jerome (following Origen and John Chrysostom) as one of the four *peccatrices*, or sinful women, in the Matthaean genealogy of Christ (Matt. 1). This sobriquet may disguise the possibility that Jerome would have described the male members of the list as *peccatores*, or sinful men, themselves. Be that as it may, the inclusion of Rahab (Josh. 2) and Bathsheba (2 Sam. 11) along with Tamar (Gen. 38) and Ruth has laid an emphasis on the supposed sexual sinfulness of the four. In fact, this is unjust and misleading. Rahab, a harlot, most often comes under discussion by exegetes because she lied in order to save the Israelites. This sin of untruth was seen as greater than her harlotry, even as she is pronounced just by St. Paul (Heb. 11). Tamar, like Ruth, is only following the dictates of the Law as, widowed, she disguises herself as a prostitute in order to trick her father-in-law into fathering a new son. The legality, indeed righteousness, of her action is recognized in the Genesis text. Ruth is always seen as blameless, since she is merely following the advice of her Jewish mother-in-law. This leaves only Bathsheba as an adulteress, but in comparison to the sins of David, hers seem rela-

tively minor. Nevertheless, this joint title has led to the women being seen as somehow especially singled-out, and carrying with them a frisson of sexual impropriety.

Certainly, there is a sexual element in Ruth. Ruth's conversation with Boaz undoubtedly has sexual overtones. But our modern ears may well tend to hear the wrong emphasis, because we associate marriage with romantic love. Ruth and Boaz are making a contract, one advantageous to both of them, in which Ruth offers herself as Boaz's wife and he gives her his protection. Sex is clearly part of the bargain, since it is Boaz's duty to father a new son; but the real scandal would be that Ruth's male relatives do not do their duty. After all, the Jewish interpretation of the story says that the unnamed relative remains unnamed precisely because he refuses to fulfill his obligation and make Ruth his wife: he is not worthy of identity. The Hebrew writer of the story does not cover up the possibility of sexual impropriety precisely in order to make his point. Boaz and Ruth remain chaste even though they have the opportunity to break that faith with the Law; but their virtue—individually and together—determines their behavior. The moral lesson is straightforward: sex is possible in many situations, but it requires the right context to make it the righteous thing to do. If Boaz had indeed been Ruth's closest relative, he could have accepted his duty and taken her as his wife there and then. But because he knew that he did not have the "right of propinquity," he acts to preserve Ruth's reputation until he can have the legal right to marry her or has seen her settled with her closer relation.

The medieval exegesis of Ruth is interesting for its decidedly Jewish slant. The linguistic difficulties of the book and the problems in understanding the ancient Hebrew customs it describes led commentators to consult Jews and Jewish commentators for enlightenment. Hebrew was understood by few Christian scholars, so they turned to their Jewish neighbors and counterparts for help. This practice was subject to much mistrust, since it needed to remain quite clear that Jews were, in the larger sense, *wrong* in their religious beliefs. Hugh of St. Cher draws a fine line when he calls the commentators he uses *Hebraei* (Hebrews) rather than *Judaei* (Jews), a distinction Christians often employed in an attempt to keep their hands clean. Nevertheless, Christian scholars realized the depth of tradition and learning of the greatest Jewish exegetes, and knew better than to disdain it. This move to consider Jewish textual traditions is not a simple matter, as is sometimes said, of a move to a more "literal" interpretation of the texts. Medieval commentators, always somewhat syncretistic, considered more important what could be got out of a text rather than how it might be done.

Ruth in the Canon

Ruth's place in the canon of Scripture, whether Hebrew or Christian, has seldom been doubted, but the exact location of the book has been in dispute. The Jewish Scriptures are divided into three parts: Law or Torah (Genesis to Deuteronomy), Prophets, and Writings or Hagiographa. One tradition puts Ruth among the Prophets, immediately after Judges. This is the position it occupies in the Septuagint and in subsequent Christian tradition, although sometimes Christians have included Ruth at the end of Judges as part and parcel of that book, just as Lamentations is sometimes counted as part of Jeremiah. The second, older tradition, which most modern scholars prefer, puts Ruth among the Writings. To begin with, this tradition put Ruth at the head of this section, preceeding the Psalms because, according to the Talmud, it was written by Samuel, who lived before David, the traditional author of the Psalms. But at some early date, Ruth was moved to become one of the five Megillot, the "little scrolls" associated with particular liturgical events. The Megillot comprise:

Song of Songs (read at Passover or Pesach);

Ruth (Feast of Weeks or Shavuot);

Ecclesiastes (Tabernacles or Sukkot);

Lamentations (the Ninth of Av or Tisha ba'Av); and

Esther (Purim).

I have given the Megillot here in their order in the Jewish year, but their arrangement has been fluid over the centuries, and this is not their order in, for example, the Masoretic text. Ruth is associated with Shavuot, which is both a harvest festival (the main action of the story takes place at the barley harvest) and also a celebration of the giving of the Law, especially to converts (Ruth is considered the convert *par excellence*). Once a year, then, Jews hear the whole story of Ruth and its interpretation.

Problems in Ruth

All of the problems raised by the medieval exegetes are still considered to be difficulties by modern scholars. Modern knowledge about, for example, semitic languages or biblical archaeology do no more than reinforce the queries or solutions in the earlier commentaries. In particular, the problem areas remain:

i)   when did the story take place? Who are the *dramatis personae*?;

ii)   what goes on at the threshing floor?;

iii) how did the sandal ceremony work?; and

iv)   what is the book for?

In addition to these large issues, some smaller points bother medieval and modern commentator alike. Why, for instance, does Naomi tell Ruth and Orpha to go back to their "mothers" instead of the expected fathers? How can Naomi be selling the field when she is said to have nothing? How big and how heavy was an ephah (how could Ruth carry it home)?

The plot of Ruth involves knowledge of two Hebrew customs. The first is "levirate marriage," the law outlined in Deut. 25:5–10, under which, if a woman is widowed without children, her husband's nearest relative is expected to marry her and father a son who will carry on her first husband's name and provide for her in her old age. This is also the principle behind the story of Tamar (Gen. 38). When Naomi sends Ruth to Boaz at the threshing floor, in order for her behavior to be justified under the Law it must be assumed that she believes Boaz to be their nearest relative, whose duty it is to take Ruth into his household, i.e., to marry her and give her a son. To understand the position properly, we must rid ourselves of anachronistic notions of romance and remember that, for most societies, marriage and families are systems of obligation and care-taking, especially for the very young and very old. For Ruth and Boaz, this marriage and its prospective children are a means of mutual care and support for all concerned.

The second custom alluded to in the story is the sandal ceremony, described in Deut. 25:8–10, which is the formal means by which the nearest relative either accepts his duty and takes the widow as his wife, or rejects her, or allows her to go with another man. The tie that binds the woman to the relative is symbolized by the thong of his sandal. If he does not wish to accept the woman, or is willing to give her away, and the woman is unhappy at this outcome, she is to pull off his sandal and spit in his face. In the Ruth story, Boaz asks the relative to take off his own sandal, symbolizing his willingly ceding his rights. Some medieval exegetes appear to find the complexities of this ritual either baffling, or perhaps too silly to bother explaining in full. The ceremony is described at some length in chapter four, but Christian commentators generally pass over it rather quickly. The Jewish commentator Josephus reports the ceremony as it should have happened, according to Deuteronomy, rather than as it appears in Ruth. For the Jews, it was important to establish the lawfulness of what Ruth and Boaz were doing. Christian authors were not interested in the scene from this legal aspect but, rather, were interested in the morality of the protagonists' behavior.

Dramatis personae

There are eight main characters (not counting Obed) in Ruth, of whom three never speak (and indeed die in the first few verses), and one is unnamed. They form a family group:

NAOMI = ELIMELECH*   UNNAMED RELATIVE
| OF ELIMELECH*
                    *(fathers were brothers)
MAALON = ORPHA   CHILION = RUTH = BOAZ
|
OBED

It is not clear why the unnamed relative was closer kin to Ruth than Boaz, unless perhaps he was the elder. In the usual Hebrew manner, their names have literal meanings, which the commentators probably got from Jerome's *Book of Interpretations of Hebrew Names*. The meanings are derived from often-obscure Hebrew but are also (in a circular rationale) inferred from the behavior and characteristics of their bearers. For example, Orpha is reckoned to mean "her neck" because, in going back to her own people, she turned the back of her neck to Ruth and Naomi, and also because she was stiff-necked in the sense of stubborn (e.g., Exod. 32:9 etc.). The names mean:

Elimelech = my God is king;
Naomi = beautiful, or a consoler;
Maalon = from a window, or from the beginning;
Chilion = consummation or burning;
Ruth = hurrying, or ceasing, or seeing;
Orpha = her neck;
Boaz = fortitude; and
Obed = serving.

The Christian exegetes add an allegorical meaning to the characters, that is, they fit the actors and their actions into a broader and more general interpretation of the story as salvation history. According to this reading, Naomi, Orpha, and Ruth represent stages in the creation of the Church. There is not, however, one single allegorical interpretation. The participants are assigned different parts depending on context. The story moves through time, so the allegories similarly shift, from pre-Christian to post-Christian times; but their movement is not a straight line. At the opening of the story, Christ has not appeared, and Naomi is the Synagogue, whose sons are kingly and priestly honor. Later she becomes the Church, whose sons are learned men. Naomi regularly shifts between being interpreted as the Synagogue and the early or primitive Church, or even the faith of that Church.

The Jews (Naomi) are living in Moab because Israel is spiritually barren—the Synagogue cannot offer them faith. Ruth and Orpha, both Moabite and therefore non-Jews in reality, represent the faithful people from among the Jews, that is, those who recognized Christ and became baptized believers. With the coming of Christ, Israel becomes fertile again. Orpha, who goes back to her old home, represents Jews who turned away from the proffered grace of or who remained stuck in the old ways of the Law.

Ruth is then also interpreted as the obedience and faith of the Gentiles (non-Jews), and she and Naomi go on to Israel, meaning that some Jews and some faithful Gentiles recognized Christ, turned to Him, and became His Church. Although they begin at different spiritual places—Naomi an Israelite and Ruth a Gentile—they both have the primary virtue of faith, and both end up as worshippers in the same Church of Christ.

The appearance of Boaz signifies the entrance of Christ. Boaz marries Ruth just as Christ marries the Church. The unnamed closer relative represents John the Baptist, who came before Christ in time but was not himself the Messiah, the Church's bridegroom.

This relatively simple allegorical reading is most easily seen in the interlinear comments of the Gloss, where the allegorical representations of each character are glossed above their names as they appear in the text, so that the text could be swiftly scanned and the Christian allegory picked up instantly by "reading between the lines."

Commentators

This section includes short notes on the commentaries I have chosen to include and the medieval authors represented in them. The choice of works is not arbitrary, although it is somewhat dictated by length. We begin with Jerome's Vulgate translation of Ruth, which appears twice, first standing alone so that readers can get to know the biblical text afresh and, second, forming the base text (the central column) of The Ordinary Gloss. Only Hugh of St. Cher, with his Paris Bible, has slight variations on this central text. Around Jerome's text range the comments of the Gloss, which I have taken from the Adolph Rusch first edition of the text (Strassburg, 1480–81) checked against a sample of Gloss manuscripts in the Bodleian Library, Oxford. The Gloss on Ruth is made up mostly of Rabanus Maurus's commentary on Ruth, with selections from the exegesis of Isidore of Seville. I have included Isidore's short text so that readers can see what was included and what omitted by the Gloss compilers. The Ordinary Gloss is twelfth century, but it acquired accretions over the years, so that, by the time it was printed, some texts were much enlarged. The additions to Ruth are particularly interesting because most of them come from the Targum Ruth (here called Chaldaeus Paraphrastes) and Theodoret—Jew and Greek—so I have included them here. Purely for ease of access, I have used the Lyons, 1589, edition. The next text is Peter Comestor's classic *Scholastic History* (*Historia scholastica*). It is followed by the two standard commentaries of their day, those of Hugh of St. Cher and Nicholas of Lyra. They represent the basic interpretation and appreciation of the text that students in theology would have known, and preached, in their academic generations and beyond.

This list of medieval exegetes, including the authors represented in the Gloss, is unusual in the amount of Jewish material it includes, but especially in the fact that it does not mention Augustine of Hippo (354–430). Medieval theology is sometimes said merely to be a footnote to Augustine, a prolific Latin author who wrote massively on virtually all aspects of Christian life and doctrine. However, Ruth contains few theological problems or doctrinal difficulties. Its problems are more those of understanding the linguistic queries and the Hebrew customs. Thus it is that the Gloss compiler did not choose to include any of Augustine's comments on Ruth, and he is not quoted by any other author.

Although Ruth is a short book, this did not necessarily inhibit the often prolix medieval author. I have chosen the authors included here not only because of their central place in medieval scholastic life but also because of their manageable size. Indeed, it may be partly because these texts were not too long that they were popular. However, the reader wishing to continue with rather longer Ruth commentaries, made for a different purpose than these scholastic texts, should consult *Commentaria in Ruth*, Corpus Christianorum Continuatio Medievalis 81 (Turnholt, 1990).

For those completely new to medieval theologians, I have included short notes on the authors represented here and, where applicable, to the particular character of their Ruth exegesis.

1. Jerome (ca. 342–420)

A biblical linguist and commentator of unsurpassed skill in his day, Jerome made new translations of the Bible from the original Greek and Hebrew. His best-known translation came to be termed the Vulgate and was the standard text in western Europe. He also composed introductory prologues to each of the biblical books or groups of books, which were the standard approaches to the overall meaning of the text. His commentaries were the norm for centuries, especially in their linguistic questions and answers. By the thirteenth century, a standard Bible, even if it contained no commentary as such, comprised Jerome's translation, with his prefaces (or those attributed to him), and his book on the interpretations of the Hebrew proper names. Jerome's translation is used here as the central text of the Bible and Ordinary Gloss sections. He appears briefly in the Additions to the Gloss to set time and place and to place Ruth in the list of four sinful women from Matthew's Gospel.

2. Isidore of Seville (ca. 560–636)

A Spanish monk and bishop known particularly for his *Etymologies*, a sort of encyclopaedia of knowledge on many subjects, arranged by definitions of key words, Isidore tried to create a compendium of the best of learning to date, but his desire for completeness means that standards of accuracy vary widely. This very completeness, however, meant that his work was very influential, and many of its explanations and definitions, however loosely based in fact, became the norm for centuries. Isidore's short treatment of Ruth here is entirely spiritually interpreted: for him, the story is simply a vehicle for a Christian allegory. Isidore's central point is to show that Christ is prefigured in the Old Testament. Nevertheless, like Peter Comestor, he keeps much of the original dialogue, and with it the original savor.

3. The Ordinary Gloss (*Glossa* or *Glossa Ordinaria*)

The Ordinary Gloss is the name generally given to the commentary on the Bible probably originating in Laon in the early twelfth century. It contained, in effect, a digest of the opinions of all the important patristic commentators, as well as some selected "moderns" on any given text, and apparently functioned as a reference work for teachers and students of biblical commentary. Quickly, it achieved something of a best-seller status, and Paris became a center for the production and distribution of manuscript copies, remarkable for their standardized layout—a central biblical text with glosses added in the margins and between the lines. There is no difference, apart from length, between the marginal and interlinear glosses; they may change places at will.

Jerome, on whose translation the Gloss's Bible text is based, is also a major source of the individual glosses, along with Ambrose, Augustine, Bede, Cassiodorus, Gregory the Great, Origen, and their ninth-century editor, Rabanus Maurus. These are the main contributors, but others, especially

Carolingian authors, are sometimes quoted on particular *lemmata*, or text-phrases.

By about 1490, it was a commonplace that the Carolingian scholars Anselm and Ralph of Laon, and Walafrid Strabo were the compilers of the Gloss, but recent scholarship prefers to credit the Psalter, Pauline Epistles, and (perhaps) the gospel of John to Anselm of Laon, and the Pentateuch, Jeremiah, and (perhaps) Joshua to 2 Kings, and the Minor Prophets to Gilbert of Auxerre, "the Universal." Anselm's brother, Ralph, may have made the Gloss on Matthew. The compiler(s) of the other Glosses remains a mystery. What is clear is that each book had a separate exegetical history, and no history or description of the Gloss as a whole can do justice to the complexity of the work without recognizing the individuality of their geneses.

The Gloss was used extensively in teaching and research by two famous Paris masters, Gilbert of Poitiers and Peter Lombard. Peter wrote commentaries on the Psalter and the Pauline Epistles which were incorporated into the glossed text as standard (the *Magna Glossatura*). The perfecting of the Gloss's characteristic layout, apparently in Paris late in the twelfth century, made it the reference tool *par excellence*.

The Glossa was printed in many early versions, the first by Adolph Rusch of Strassburg (1480–81). From the 1495 edition onwards, the Gloss was often printed together with the *postillae* of Nicholas of Lyra, but after about 1500 an increasing number of interpolations in the printed texts make them unreliable witnesses to the twelfth-century versions.

Ruth in the Gloss

Almost the entire Ruth Gloss is taken from Rabanus Maurus's (776/84–856) *Commentary on Ruth* [*PL* 108:1199C–1224A]. A few of the extra phrases are not from Rabanus, and the meanings of the Hebrew names, especially those in the genealogy at the end of chapter four, are from Jerome's *Book of Interpretations of Hebrew Names.*

Rabanus (sometimes Hrabanus) was a highly influential theologian, poet, and churchman who held the offices of Abbot of Fulda and Archbishop of Mainz. As well as biblical exegesis, he wrote manuals for the clergy and a quasi-encyclopaedia, "On the Nature of Things," which continued the mystical interpretation of the world promoted in his biblical work.

The Gloss is rarely taken from Rabanus verbatim but is usually abbreviated and paraphrased, often quite heavily. Rabanus often begins his comments with questions, which the Gloss turns into statements. These transformations can make the Latin of the text somewhat hard to fathom, especially when the compiler contracts several sentences into one, with a number of sub-clauses more or less obviously dependent on the main subject. Latin syntax makes it rather simpler to understand the structure of the sentences than English—more reliant on word order—can briefly do. Yet I have tried to retain at least some of the Latin flavor, so that students can get a sense of the language and method of the Gloss. We have no real idea of who might have compiled the Ruth section of the Gloss.

The Ruth Gloss consists of short allegorical readings, as well as simply glossing difficult words and adding brief explanations of opaque phrases. There is no single line running throughout the Gloss; rather, it is a series of changing allegories, containing a fluidity of imagery that marks much medieval exegesis. The trinity of Naomi, Ruth, and Orpha varies their meaning, with Naomi as both the Synagogue and the Church (and sometimes "the faith of the Church"), Ruth as faithful Jews and obedient Gentiles, and Orpha as both Jewish and a baptized believer. Modern readers may find the shifting sands confusing and treacherous—we are never quite sure we are putting our feet on firm ground; but for medieval exegetes this variety only signalled more possible uses for the material, and they were happier to leap between stepping stones, supplying the rest of the path in their own heads.

The Gloss interpretation is not anti-Jewish, simply totally Christian, since its allegorical intent ignores most of the Jewish character. It may be summed up in one of its own phrases: the exegesis of the Gloss is intended to illuminate "the spiritual lineage of the race."

4. Chaldaeus Paraphrastes

"The Chaldean paraphrase" is the phrase used by the Gloss Additions to refer to the Jewish Targum, that is, the Aramaic (i.e., Chaldean) translations or paraphrases made of the Hebrew Bible (Old Testament) when Hebrew was no longer the everyday language of the Jews and could not be understood by most listeners in synagogue. The Targums were the oral interpretations of the biblical text, used in the synagogue; the earliest date from at least the first century A.D., although the Ruth Targum is hard to date and is thought to be later.

All the Targum to the Megillot (Ruth, Esther, Ecclesiastes, Song of Songs, Lamentations) are similar in being not simply translations but also paraphrases of the text with exegetical elements built in, although some of the difficult Hebrew constructions do make their way verbatim into the Targum text, which probably accounts for why the Latin translation can be so opaque.

As it appears in the Additions, the Targum is interested in righteousness, that is, adherence to the Law and its reward, and unrighteousness and its consequences. Thus it tries to explain why the unfortunate things in the story happen, as well as the good, and its comments are often of the "this was on account of" variety. And so it is in order to establish the position of the characters vis-à-vis the Law that the Targum asks questions about the literal sense of the text. The Targum is the most common source of the Gloss Additions; how it found its way into the Gloss text is still a matter for research.

5. Josephus (ca. 37–ca. 100)

Josephus was a Palestinian Jew who, having taken part in the Jewish wars, surrendered to the Romans and became a Roman citizen, with a pension that allowed him to practice his craft as an historian. His two great works, the *The Wars of the Jews* and *The Antiquities of the Jews* were mined by early Christian writers for historical material. He appears very little in the Gloss Additions, simply to add explanations of a few words.

6. John Chrysostom (ca. 347–407)

A monk and bishop of Constantinople, Chrysostom ("golden mouthed") was especially famous for his homilies. He was an enthusiast for the literal interpretation of Scripture against allegories. The Gloss on Ruth uses both genuine Chrysostom homilies on Matthew as well as the spurious *Opus Imperfectum*, an incomplete second series of homilies on Matthew widely attributed to him. In fact, the *Opus* was probably the work of a fifth-century Arian scholar. Both real and pseudo-Chrysostom are used in the Gloss Additions to ask *why* Boaz married Ruth, by considering what traits are praiseworthy in them both.

7. Theodoret (ca. 393–ca. 466)

Greek monk and bishop of Cyrrhus, Theodoret attended the crucial early Church councils at Ephesus (431) and Chalcedon (451), where he was on the losing side of the Christological debate with Cyril of Alexandria. Little of his work remains to us, but what there is shows him as a fine biblical exegete, early Apologist, and Church historian. He appears surprisingly often in the Gloss Additions, on the issue of what should be admired in Ruth and Boaz, and on the rewards given to the virtuous.

8. Ambrose (ca. 339–397)

Bishop of Milan famous for being acclaimed bishop by the Milanese laity when still unbaptized. He was known in the Middle Ages for his Letters, and his works *On the Sacraments*, *On Virginity*, and *On the Offices the Church*. He is, unusually, little-used in the Gloss on Ruth, being simply quoted on widowhood, which he counted as one of the forms of virginity. The Gloss Additions use Ambrose to comment on the goodness of Ruth's and Naomi's souls.

9. Peter Comestor (d. ca. 1179)

A French biblical scholar and chancellor of the University of Paris, Peter is best-known as the author of the *Scholastic History* (*Historia scholastica*), a history of the biblical period (mostly focusing on the Old Testament) based closely on Scripture but with interpolations from patristic and pagan writers. The *History* was an immense success, forming as it does a clear, simple, more coherent narrative than the Bible itself, ironing out textual difficulties and yet retaining much of the dialogue and flavor of the original. It provides all the essentials of the Bible, in the format of edited highlights.

Peter's treatment of Ruth is even shorter and more compressed than the original, but he maintains the conversations between Ruth and Naomi, and Ruth and Boaz, on top of the bones of the story. Peter also attempts to sort out the custom of untying the sandal. His treatment relies heavily on Josephus, especially on questions of literal sense. We can feel the pressure of student questions driving his comments throughout.

10. Hugh of St. Cher (ca. 1200–1263)

A Dominican from the St. Jacques convent in Paris, Hugh was the greatest Bible commentator of his generation. As well as glossing the entire Bible, Hugh was responsible for a team of Dominican scholars who produced a series of reader-aids in books aimed particularly at preachers. They compiled indexes, concordances, cross-references, textual correction, and Bibles in handy pocket-sized format. All his work was aimed at making the latest scholarship easily accessible to preachers in the field.

His commentary on Ruth is very much indebted to Stephen Langton (biblical scholar and archbishop of Canterbury, d. 1228), both in ideas and paraphrased commentary. He also includes much of the Gloss, without direct attribution—a common practice with such a universal source. He divides his commentary into literal and spiritual senses, although his literal interpretation includes much that is allegorical. The commentary rests on lemmata, which renders it disjointed and variable in depth and fluency, although the tone is much more scholarly, or rather classroom, than any of the previous commentators. Hugh fills in much detail, considering the text at some length, and employs an impressive array of biblical quotation.

The spiritual interpretation tries to sort out the various allegorical readings of the text. Hugh gives his own, as well as repeating those in the Gloss. He uses this sense very much as a lesson to his own day, leaving us with one side of some fascinating arguments. He particularly highlights for us the infighting between the secular doctors and the Friars preaching in the field, and is careful to distinguish between school-learning and wisdom. His spiritual interpretation covers the contents of all three of the theoretical spiritual levels: deeds, beliefs, and the life of the world to come. Hugh is clear, straightforward, and practical, leaving a strong impression of a bracing teacher.

11. Nicholas of Lyra (ca. 1270–1340)

Nicholas was a Franciscan master at Paris notable for his knowledge of Hebrew and of Jewish exegesis, especially that of Rashi (Rabbi Solomon ben Isaac [1040–1105] of Troyes, whose highly influential biblical commentary concentrated on understanding the literal meaning of the text). Like Hugh of St. Cher, Nicholas commented on the entire Bible, was the chief exegete of his age, and his commentaries were the first to be printed (Rome, 1471–72). His work exhibits curiosity and exactitude of mind, seen in his need for comprehension of the literal meaning of Scripture before moving on to a spiritual exegesis.

Nicholas concentrates heavily on the literal sense of the text, although this encompasses much that might elsewhere be seen as spiritual. To aid him in this, he draws heavily on Jewish sources, mainly through Rashi's Ruth commentary. He makes many positive comments on the sense and correctness of the "Hebrew" expositors over some earlier Christian interpretation. Nicholas is very much concerned with the truth or falsity of the text, desiring to show that the literal meaning can, even in its detail, teach us much that will strengthen our faith. His distinctiveness is in his conviction that the literal text must be able to make sense to Christians, and speak to their faith. Comparatively, his treatment of the spiritual sense is slight, perhaps because he felt that others had addressed these issues: he could find his niche in the rather neglected literal. His commentary style is detailed and somewhat laborious—undoubtedly he likes the reader to "see the working," and follow the argument through to the end. This does not leave him with a reputation for elegance, but the scholarship is admirable, nonetheless.

Sources

A brief list outlining sources used by each commentary:

	Direct Scriptural refs. (OT / NT)	Non-biblical refs
Isidore	4 (0 / 4)	0
Gloss	59 (22 / 37)	0 (not Rabanus)
Additions	0	34
Comestor	2 (1 / 1)	3
Hugh	104 (51 / 53)	11
Nicholas	32 (24 / 8)	17 (not Rashi)

Medieval Biblical Commentary

On the Method of Commentary

The exegeses included in this selection all follow the common pattern of selecting a *lemma* (a word or phrase) and making comments on it. These comments take different forms. They may be a gloss (explanation) of a single word, a rephrasing of a difficult construction, information giving the background to an ancient custom, the Christianizing of a Jewish text, an interpretation to give a passage a moral meaning, a flashback or forward to link a character or event with others in the Bible, or a reflection of the Old Testament in the New. Clearly some of these forms vary in intent: what the commentator means to achieve by them is very different. The "classical" medieval theory of exegesis is usually stated by modern scholars in the form (probably) given it by Augustine of Dacia, and often repeated in various forms:

Littera gesta docet, quid credas allegoria,
Moralis quid agas, quo tendas anagogia.

The literal sense teaches you about deeds,
The allegorical teaches what you should believe,
The moral teaches what you should do,
The anagogical shows where you should be aiming.

The standard scholastic theory, then, was that Scripture could be interpreted four ways, according to the four "senses" of this verse, each sense highlighting one aspect of understanding for the believer. In its first printed version, in the prologues to Nicholas of Lyra's *postillae* on Scripture (Rome, 1471–72), the verse is followed by an example: Nicholas interprets "Jerusalem" according to the four senses. Literally Jerusalem is the earthly city of ancient Israel, morally it is the faithful soul (Isai. 52:2, "Rise up, O captive Jerusalem"), allegorically it is the Church militant (Rev. 21:2, "And I saw the holy city, the new Jerusalem"), and anagogically it is the Church triumphant (Gal. 4:26, "The Jerusalem above . . .

she is our mother"). So ran the theory, and it is interesting that, certainly by the thirteenth century, it was felt necessary to have a theory. How much it was applied in practice is another matter. Most of our commentators make their exegesis as a piece, using whatever interpretations seem to them most apt at the time. Hugh of St. Cher and Nicholas of Lyra do divide their commentaries into parts, or senses, but, as is generally the case, they use only two, literal and spiritual. The spiritual sense is named *allegorice*, *mystice*, or *moraliter*, interchangeably it would seem. And indeed, since these sorts of headings are likely to be the decision of the scribe or reporter or printer of the text, the exact word may not be original to the author, in any case; the point is simply to signal to the reader that we have passed from one type of interpretation to another.

Even so, the literal–spiritual divide is not as clear cut as it might at first seem, for the meaning of "literal" (or "historical") in these terms was a variable and now-debated issue, encompassing much, from the straightforward "meaning of the words" to the full intention of the author, however "spiritual" that may have been. This last was particularly the case when a sentence seemed so opaque as to have no "real" meaning at all: its literal sense must needs be a spiritual interpretation. In the end, medieval exegetes believed, in Nicholas of Lyra's words, that Sacred Scripture was about "true understanding and good doing." They would elicit any possible meaning from the text that would provide the faithful with edifying teaching towards those ends.

On Medieval Latin Biblical Citations

Since the majority of biblical books are named after individuals, their titles are very similar in Latin and English, and easily recognizable. However, the titles of some books are translations of their meanings and can be confusing. Beginners might wish to note: *Iudices* (Judges); *Paralipomenon* (Chronicles); *Canticum Canticorum* (Song of Songs); *Sapientia* (Wisdom); *Threni* (Lamentations); *Sirach* (Ecclesiasticus); and *Apocalysum* (Revelation). Samuel and Kings, with two books each in the English listing, form in Latin four books of Kings (*Regum*), so that 1 Sam. becomes 1 *Reg.*, and 1 Kings becomes 3 *Reg.* The numbering of the psalms and their verses, as well as the Latin translation used, can often be a stumbling block, since three translations (Roman, Gallican, Hebrew) were in circulation. Generally speaking, between psalms 10 and 148, the numbering of modern English psalters is one psalm ahead of the medieval numbering, with some possible differences in verse numbers where the psalms' titles are included in the numbering.

Most of the biblical references in these texts are given by book and chapter only (exact and standardized biblical references do not become common until the thirteenth century). For convenience, I have added the verse reference (where possible) in the text itself.

Similarly, the order of medieval Bibles may differ from our standard Bibles today, just as Bibles from the Roman Catholic and Protestant traditions differ (with Protestant Bibles sometimes including the books of the Apocrypha), or Hebrew Bibles contain books in a different order from the Christian Old Testament.

On the Standardization of the Spelling of Names

Consistency of spelling was not counted among medieval virtues, and where foreign words were concerned that trait was heightened. Spelling followed local pronunciation or custom, so there are variations from scribe to scribe and place to place. Students approaching these texts will find themselves faced with a variety of possibilities, sometimes varying within a text. In Ruth, the commonest variants are Beth-Leem, Noemi, Ruht (probably reflecting pronunciation), Bo-oz, Mahlon, Kilion, Aod or Aioth (for Ehud), Phares (Perez), Isai (Jesse). For convenience, I have used the spellings of the New Revised Standard Version of the Bible.

A Note on the Translation

Wherever possible, I have kept the translation close to the Latin, so that students can get the flavor of the original. However, there are some conventions, especially in the Gloss, that I have softened, such as the use of sentences beginning "vel" (or) or "quia" (because). In the syntax of the Gloss, these are shorthand for, "In another interpretation, this means . . ." and "This is said because . . ." or similar phrases. I have also tried to smooth out those comments which seem to carry on and complete a short lemma, as though completing a sentence in a different way, and those which are detached from the lemma and try to interpret the meaning of the whole phrase or idea that it conveys. The Latin of these glosses tends towards one long sentence divided into several subclauses, or to chains of clauses joined by "and." On the whole, I have divided these into shorter sentences, although some have been left, either for authenticity or because division would take us very far from the original Latin. Simultaneously, exegetical style can be both rambling and compressed.

I have used capitals in referring to God and Christ (and He and His, etc.) not for any religious reason but to make the reference of the text as clear as possible. Italics show direct quotations, usually from the Bible. Quotation marks designate a piece of invented dialogue; where this incorporates a biblical quotation, italics are used inside quotation marks.

Abbreviations and Editions of Texts Used

PL = J.-P. Migne, *Patrologiae Latinae*, 221 vols. and Supplement (Paris, 1844–63).
PG = J.-P. Migne, *Patrologiae Graecae*, 161 vols. (Paris, 1857–66).
Although elderly and not always reliable, the Migne *Patrologia* series of editions is often still the only printed source of many patristic works, or at least the only easily available source.

Ambrose, *Commentarius in Lucam*, ed. I. Tissot, Sources Chrétiennes no. 45 (Paris, 1956).

Ambrose, *Liber de viduis*, PL 16:233–262.

Biblia sacra, cum glossa ordinaria . . . et postilla Nicolai Lyrani (Lyons, 1589). Used for The Ordinary Gloss, the Gloss Additions, and Nicholas of Lyra's Postills.

Biblia Latina cum glossa ordinaria, facsimile edition, ed. Adolph Rusch (Strassburg, 1480/81).

Chaldaeus Paraphrastes (the *Targum Ruth*):
SO = A. Saarisalo, "The Targum to the book of Ruth," in *Studia Orientalia*, 2 (1928), 88–104;
AB = E. Levine, "The Aramaic version of Ruth," *Analecta Biblica* 58 (Rome, 1973).
The latter is a translation with textual and contexual study, and a good bibliography.

Hugh of St. Cher, *Pars . . . bibliae cum postilla . . . Hugonis* (Paris, 1533).

Jerome, *Quaestiones Hebraicae in libros regum et Paralipomenon*, PL 23:1329–1402.

Jerome, *Commentaire sur S. Matthieu*, ed. E. Bonnard, Sources Chrétiennes nos. 242, 259 (Paris, 1977–79).

Jerome, *Letters*, no. 39, to Paula: *Epitaph Blesilae*, Corpus Scriptorum Ecclesiasticorum Latinorum 54, pp. 293–308.

John Chrysostom, *Homeliae in Matthaeum*, PG 57–58.

Ps.-John Chrysostom, *Opus Imperfectum* ("Eruditi commentarii in evangelium Matthaei, incerto auctore"), *PG* 56:611–946.

Josephus, *The Antiquities of the Jews*, trans. W. Whiston (London, 1963).

Rashi, *Commentary on Ruth*, in J. F. Breithaupt, *R. Salomonis Jarehi . . . Commentarius Hebraicus in Lib. Joshuae . . . Canticum Canticorum etc.* (Gotha, 1714).

Theodoret, *Quaestiones in Ruth*, *PG* 80:517–528.

Some Further Reading

Straightforward beginners books on medieval exegesis are sadly lacking. The following list includes the few classics and one or two useful modern additions:

The Cambridge History of the Bible, vol. 2: *The West from the Fathers to the Reformation*, ed. G. W. Lampe (Cambridge, 1969), esp. chap. VI.

R. Gameson, ed., *The Early Medieval Bible* (Cambridge, 1994).

H. de Lubac, *Exégèse médiévale: Les quatre sens de l'Ecriture*, 4 vols. (Paris, 1959–64). The "spiritual sense," somewhat in contrast to Smalley's pro-literal view.

E. Ann Matter, *The Voice of My Beloved: The Song of Songs in Western Medieval Christianity* (Philadelphia, 1990), esp. first three chapters for general interpretation.

O. Lottin, *Psychologie et morale aux xiie et xiiie siècles*, 5 vols. (Louvain-Gembloux, 1942–60). Classic, comprehensive reference work.

B. Smalley, *The Study of the Bible in the Middle Ages*, 3rd ed. (Oxford, 1982). The English standard; anything by Smalley is learned and insightful.

P. C. Spicq, *Esquisse d'une histoire de l'exégèse latine au moyen âge* (Paris, 1944).

Facsimile reprint of the Rusch 1480–81 edition of *Biblia Latina cum Glossa Ordinaria*, ed. K. Froehlich and M. Gibson (Turnhout, 1992).

Encyclopaedia Judaica, 16 vols. (Jerusalem, 1971).

H. Hailperin, *Rashi and the Christian Scholars* (Pittsburgh, 1963). Disappointing; but there is little to compare it with.

Andreae de Sancto Victore Opera: Expositionem in Ezechielem, ed. M. A. Signer, Corpus Christianorum Continuatio Medievalis (Turnhout, 1991). English introduction considers medieval Jewish-Christian scholarly relations.

Modern commentaries on Ruth can be found in a number of modern exegetical series, such as the Anchor Bible, vol. 7, ed. E. F. Campbell, *Ruth: A New Translation with Introduction, Notes and Commentary* (Garden City, N.Y., 1975). The *New Jerome Bible Commentary*, ed. R. Brown, J. Fitzmyer, and R. Murphy (London, 1990), gives a brief but solid outline of exegesis for each book, with bibliography.

Jerome: The Book of Ruth

Chapter 1

In the days of a certain judge, when judges ruled,[1] there was a famine in the land. And[2] a man went out from Bethlehem of Judah into exile[3] in the country of the Moabites, with his wife and two sons. And he was called Elimelech, and his wife was Naomi, and two sons, one Maalon, the other Chilion, Ephrathites of Bethlehem of Judah. And having come to the country of the Moabites, they stayed there. And Elimelech, Naomi's husband, died, and she was left with her sons. They took Moabite wives, one of whom was called Orpha, and the other Ruth. And so they continued there for ten years, and both died, that is, Maalon and Chilion; and the woman was left, deprived of her two sons and her husband.

And she arose in order to start for her native land from the Moabite country, with both her daughters-in-law; for she had heard that the Lord had looked after his own people and had given them food. Therefore she set out from the place of her exile with both daughters-in-law, and when they were already on the road which would take them back to the land of Judah, she said to them, "Go home to your mothers; may the Lord have mercy on you, just as you had mercy on my dead family, and on me. May the Lord grant that you find rest in the houses of men that you choose." And she kissed them. And, raising their voices, they began to weep and said, "We will go with you to your people." She answered them, "Go back, my daughters. Why come with me? Do I have more sons in my womb that you may hope for husbands from me? Turn back, my daughters, and leave me, for I am already an old woman, not suited to the bonds of marriage; even if I were able to conceive this very night and bear sons, if you wished to wait for them until they grew up and completed the years of puberty, you would be old women before you were married. I pray you not to stay, my daughters, because your difficulty oppresses me more than it does you, and the hand of the Lord is turned against me." And raising their voices, again they began to cry. Orpha kissed her mother-in-law and turned back; Ruth stuck by her mother-in-law. Naomi said to her, "Look! Your sister has gone back to her people and to her gods: go with her." She answered, "Do not oppose me to make me leave you and go away. I shall go wherever you go; I shall stay wherever you stay. Your people are my people, and your God is my God. Whatever earth receives you when you die, I shall die there and I shall be buried there. May the Lord do these things for me, and let him add things, if even death separates me and you." Therefore, seeing that Ruth had made up her mind and had decided to go with her, Naomi was not willing to resist her nor to persuade her to return to her own people; and they went on together and came to Bethlehem.

When they had entered the town, knowledge of them spread swiftly to all, and the women said, "This is Naomi herself." But she answered, "Call me not Naomi (that is, beautiful), but call me Mara (that is, bitterness) because the Almighty has filled me greatly with bitterness. I set out full and the Lord has led me back empty. Why then call me Naomi, whom the Lord has brought low and the Almighty has afflicted?" Thus Naomi came with Ruth, the Moabite woman, her daughter-in-law, from the land of her exile; and she came back into Bethlehem when the first barley was being harvested.

Chapter 2

But there was a kinsman of the man Elimelech, a man of power and of great wealth, Boaz by name.

Ruth, the Moabite woman, said to her mother-in-law, "If you agree, I will go into a field and collect the gleanings which have escaped the hands of the reapers, wherever I meet with kindness from a merciful landowner." She answered her, "Go, my daughter; go, indeed, and collect the grain behind the backs of the reapers." It happened, however, that the field was owned by Boaz, who was a kinsman of Elimelech. And behold, he came from Bethlehem, and he said to the reapers, "The Lord be with you." They answered him, "May the Lord bless you." And Boaz said to the young man who was in charge of the reapers, "Who does this girl belong to?" He answered, "She is a Moabite woman who came with Naomi from the country of the Moabites, and she asked if she might collect the leftover grain, following in the footsteps of the harvesters; and from early this morning till now she has stood in the field, and not gone home, even for a moment." And Boaz said to Ruth, "Hear me, daughter. Do not go to another field to collect the grain, nor leave here: but join my young girls, and where they reap the grain, follow them. For I have given orders to my young men that no-one should bother you: and if you are thirsty, go to my baggage and drink the water which the young people drink." And she, falling on her face on the ground and revering him, said to him, "Why have I found favor in your sight, that you should think me, a foreign woman, worthy?" He answered her, "Everything has been reported to me: what you did for your mother-in-law after the death of her husband, and that you abandoned your parents and the land where you were born and came to this people which you did not previously know. The Lord repays you for your deeds, and you shall receive full reward from the Lord God of Israel, to whom you came, and under whose wings you flew." And she said, "I have found favor in your sight, my Lord, who has comforted me, and who has spoken to the heart of your handmaiden, as though I were like one of your girls, which I am not." And Boaz said to her, "When it is evening, come here and eat the bread and dip your morsel in the vinegar."

And so she sat beside the reapers and he col-

lected barley-flour for her, and she ate and was satisfied and took the rest away. And from then on it became the custom for her to collect the grain. Indeed, Boaz commanded his boys, saying, "Even should she wish to reap with you, do not prevent her, and even throw out grain from your bundles on purpose and leave it there, so that she may glean without shame; and no-one should reprove her for gleaning." Accordingly, she collected grain in the field until the evening, and cutting and shaking out what she had collected with a rod, she found it was an ephah's worth of barley, that is, three measures. Carrying this, she went back to the city and showed her mother-in-law; on top of this she brought out and gave her the rest of her meal, so that she was made full.[4]

And her mother-in-law said to her, "Where did you glean today, and where did you do this work? May he who was merciful to you be blessed." And she told her about how she had been treated, and said the man's name, that he was called Boaz. And Naomi replied, "May he be blessed by the Lord, since he has performed a service for the dead with the same kindness which he has shown to the living." And again she said, "Our neighbor is a true man." And Ruth said, "He also ordered me to join in with his reapers until all the fields were reaped." Her mother-in-law said to her, "My daughter, it is better for you to go out to reap with his girls, in case someone stops you gleaning in another field." And so she joined herself to Boaz's girls, and reaped with them until the barley and wheat were stored in the granaries.

Chapter 3

When, however, she returned to her mother-in-law, she was told by her, "My daughter, I will try to get you rest and provide for your welfare. This Boaz, whose girls you joined in the field, is our relative, and tonight he winnows the grain on the threshing floor of the granary. Wash yourself, therefore, and anoint yourself, and put on your best clothes, and go down to the threshing floor. The man may not see you until he has finished eating and drinking. But when he leaves to go to sleep, take note of the place where he sleeps, and go and turn back that part of the blanket covering his feet, and slip yourself underneath, and lie there. He will tell you what you should do."[5] And she answered, "I will do whatever you order."

And she went down to the threshing floor, and did all that her mother-in-law had ordered her. And when Boaz had eaten and drunk and had made merry, and had left to go to sleep next to the pile of hay, she came secretly and turned back the blanket covering his feet and slipped herself underneath it. And behold, in the middle of the night, the man was afraid and was perturbed: and he saw the woman lying at his feet and said to her, "Who are you?" And she answered, "I am Ruth, your handmaid. Spread your blanket over your servant, because you are her kinsman." And he said, "Daughter, you are blessed by the Lord, and you have surpassed your former pity with your latest pity, because you have not run after young men, poor or rich. Do not be afraid, therefore; but what you have asked me, I shall do for you. For everyone who lives within the gates of my city knows you to be a woman of virtue. I do not deny that you are my relative; but there is someone who is a closer relative to you than me. Stay here tonight, and in the morning, if he wishes to preserve the law of propinquity,[6] all well and good; but if he does not wish it, I will receive you into my household without any hesitation, as the Lord lives. Sleep until morning."

And so she slept at his feet till daylight. And she arose before men knew each other, and Boaz said, "Take care, in case anyone knows that you came here." And again he said, "Stretch out the blanket which covers you and hold it in both hands." As she held it outstretched he measured out six measures of barley and placed it on the blanket. Carrying this, she went into the city and went to her mother-in-law, who said to her, "What did you do, daughter?" And she told her everything that the man had done for her. And she said,

"Behold, he gave me six measures of barley, and he said, 'I do not want you to return to your mother-in-law empty[-handed]'."[7] And Naomi said, "Just wait, daughter, and see what the outcome will be. For the man will not rest until he has done what he said."

Chapter 4

Boaz went up to the town gate and sat there. And when he saw his relative (whom he had spoken of earlier), go past, he said to him, calling him by his name,[8] "Pause a little while, and sit here." And he paused and sat down. Then Boaz, bringing over ten men from amongst the town elders, said to them, "Sit down here." And when they were settled, he said to his neighbor, "Naomi, who returned from the country of the Moabites, is selling part of the field belonging to our brother Elimelech. I wished you to hear this and to tell you this in front of the whole seated assembly and elders of my people. If you wish to have the field, buy it and have it, by the law of propinquity. However, if you do not want it, tell me, so I know what I should do. For there is no nearer relative than you who have priority, and I who am second." Whereupon he replied, "I will buy the field." To which Boaz said, "When you buy the field from the woman's hand, you must also take on Ruth, the Moabite woman whose husband is dead, to keep alive the name[9] of your relative in your heredity." To which he replied, "I cede my right by the law of propinquity; for I should not harm the future of my family. You may have my privilege, which I declare that I give up freely."

Now this, indeed, was the ancient custom in Israel amongst kinsmen, that whenever anyone ceded his right under the law to another, so that it was conceded definitely, the man undid his own sandal and gave it to his neighbor.[10] In Israel, this was proof of the giving up of the right. Boaz therefore said to his neighbor, "Take off your sandal." And he immediately undid his sandal. And he said, before the elders and all the people,

"You are witnesses today that I will take over all the things which belonged to Elimelech and Chilion and Maalon, handed down to Naomi; and Ruth, the Moabite woman, the wife of Maalon, I will take in marriage, and I will revive the name of the dead in her children, so that his name of his [Elimelech's] family and brothers will not be lost amongst the people. I call you as witnesses of this act." All the people who were at the gate and the elders answered, "We are witnesses; the Lord made this woman, who has come into your house, like Rachel and Leah, who built the house of Israel, so that she may be an example of virtue in Ephrathah, and she may have a name famous throughout Bethlehem. And may your house be [established] from the seed which the Lord will have given to you from this girl, as was the house of Perez, whom Tamar bore of Judah."

And so Boaz took Ruth and made her his wife; and he went in to her and the Lord made her conceive and bear a son. And the women said to Naomi, "Blessed be the Lord who has not allowed your family to die out, and his name will be known in Israel. And you have someone to console your spirit, and to care for you in your old age. For he is born from your daughter-in-law who loves you, and he is far better for you than if you had seven sons." And Naomi took the child and placed it on her bosom and acted as his nurse and nanny. And, indeed, the neighborhood women congratulated her, saying, "A son is born to Naomi." They named him Obed. He was the father of Jesse the father of David. These are the generations of Perez: Perez fathered Hezron, Hezron fathered Ram, Ram fathered Amminadab, Amminadab fathered Nahshon, Nahshon fathered Salmon, Salmon fathered Boaz, Boaz fathered Obed, Obed fathered Jesse, Jesse fathered David.

Translated from *PL* 28:543–48.

Notes

1. "Taken in combination, the five Hebrew words at the start of Ruth show unique syntax," E. F. Campbell, *Ruth* (Anchor Bible, 7; Garden City, N.Y., 1975), p. 49. This problematical Hebrew explains why the first sentence varies so much in translations. However, it is clear that the writer means to set the story at a particular point in the past, establishing a kind of historical veracity.

2. "And" is the most common Hebrew connective. Whereas English might use a variety of "but," "however," "although," etc., Hebrew simply joins one thought to another, leaving the context to make the meaning clear. These "ands," which Jerome translated literally, add to the sense of movement and press of events in chapter 1: one thing follows closely on another.

3. "Peregrinatio," which also means pilgrimage. "Pilgrimage" and "exile" provide a slight play on words throughout the text.

4. This refers back to—and reverses—Naomi's statement to the women, in chapter 1: "I set out full and the Lord has led me back empty."

5. The somewhat ambiguous sense of what is actually going to happen here is undoubtedly intended by the author. He heightens the tension in the passage by using a number of Hebrew sexual euphemisms, most notably "feet," which could also mean "genitals." The anxiety is meant not to titillate the reader but to show how Ruth and Boaz *might* have behaved had they not chosen the virtuous route. For further discussion, see Campbell, *Ruth*, pp. 121, 130–32.

6. The law of propinquity, or of the closer relation, refers to the institution of "levirate marriage" described in Deut. 25:5–10. If a woman were widowed, without a male heir, it was her husband's closest relative's duty to marry her and conceive a son, who would both carry on his father's name and provide for his mother. See further T. Thompson and D. Thompson, "Some Legal Problems in the Book of Ruth," *Vetus Testamentum* 18 (1968), 79–99.

7. Note once again the references to empty and full in chaps. 1 and 2. Ruth goes to Boaz empty but he sends her back to Naomi full. Later, she will be "full" with his child. Most importantly, the Israelites begin the story empty—in exile from their land because of a famine, with no sense of future—and end it triumphantly full, back in Israel with the promise of King David to come.

8. Although Boaz called him by his name, we are not told what this was. The Hebrew tradition says that, because the man was not willing to do his duty by Ruth, he was not worthy to be named.

9. "Name": literally "seed."

10. Jerome's translation is clear here: the man undoes his own (*suum*) sandal. Other writers lost the reflexive pronoun, letting in much confusion about who was to do what to whom.

Isidore of Seville: On Ruth

Now let us look at Ruth, for she is a "type" of the Church.[1] First she is a type because she is a stranger from the Gentile people who renounced her native land and all things belonging to it. She made her way to the land of Israel. And when her mother-in-law forbade her from coming with her she persisted, saying, "Wherever you go, I shall go; your people shall be my people; and your God shall be my God. Whichever land receives you as you die, there I too shall die." This voice without doubt shows that she is a type of the Church.

For the Church was called to God from the Gentiles in just this way: leaving her native land (which is idolatry) and giving up all earthly associations, she confessed that He in whom the saints believed is the Lord God; and that she herself will go where the flesh of Christ ascended after His passion; and that on account of His name she would suffer in this world unto death; and that she will unite with the community of the saints, that is, the patriarchs and prophets. This company, by virtue of which she [Ruth] might be joined to the longed-for saints from the lineage of Abraham, Moses revealed to us in the canticle, saying, "Rejoice, you nations, with his people, (that is, people of the Gentiles), pour forth what you believe; exult with those who were first chosen for eternal joy" (Rom. 15:10). When Ruth entered the land of Israel with her mother-in-law, it was provided (on account of the merits of her prayers) that she be married to a man of the lineage of Abraham, and whom, indeed, she at first believed to be her closest kinsman. He said that he could not marry her and, when he had withdrawn, Boaz was married to her, with the witness of ten elders. He who previously confessed himself unable to marry that same woman was united with her, and was blessed by those ten elders.

It is thought that this passage prefigures John the Baptist who, when he himself was thought by the people of Israel to be Christ and was asked who he was, did not deny who he was, but confessed it, saying that he was not Christ. And those who were sent persisted in these inquiries about who he was. He answered, "I am the voice crying in the desert" (John 1:19–27). He confessed the good news about the Lord, saying, "He who has the bride is the bridegroom." He showed that he himself was the friend of the groom [best man], since he added, "Truly, the friend of the groom is he who stands and hears him and rejoices on account of the groom's voice" (John 3:28–29). And so they thought he was Christ, because they did not understand that Christ had come on the day of the Visitation (Luke 1:40–45), and that he who was earlier promised by the prophets' voices was the Church's bridegroom. But just as he told her he was not her kinsman, but then afterwards Ruth was united with Boaz, so Christ, who is the true bridegroom of the Church, whom the sayings of all the prophets proclaim, was deemed worthy, from all Gentile nations, to claim the Church, to present to God the Father unnumbered people throughout the whole orb of the world, because his kinsman took off his sandals.

It was an old custom that if a groom wished to divorce his bride he took off his sandal, and this was the sign of the divorce. Consequently, he was ordered to take off his sandals, lest he approach the Church wearing sandals like a bridegroom; for this office was reserved for Christ, who is the true bridegroom. However, the blessing of the ten elders showed that all Gentile peoples were saved and blessed in the name of Christ. For iota signifies ten in Greek, and this first letter will signify the name of the Lord Jesus in full; which shows, as we said, that all peoples are saved through him, and are blessed. Therefore, let no one doubt these things that were said, since it may be seen that they were everywhere and from the beginning prefigured by antecedent figures; and they were clearly fulfilled in this way through the advent of the Lord; and which were superfluous, being completed in this way by the accord of all voices in truth; and by all "figures" of the holy scriptures, which He who promised [them] fulfilled through His son, Jesus Christ our Lord, king, and redeemer and savior, with whom is honor and glory from age to age. Amen.

Translated from Oxford, Bodleian Library, MS Add. C. 16, fol. 98r–v, collated with London, BL, MS Royal 3 A.VII, fol. 65r–v.

Notes

1. By "type" or typology, Isidore and other patristic and medieval exegetes mean a signification—something symbolized or (pre-) figured by something else. Christian exegesis often sees an Old Testament person, object, or event as prefiguring some person or object in the New Testament or in the Church. The Old is seen as a "type" of the New.

The Ordinary Gloss

CHAPTER 1

^a of princes of this world

In the days of a certain judge, when judges^a

^b the Synagogue ^c of the Word ^d on the earth

ruled,^b there was a famine^c in the land.^d And

^e Christ ^f was born ^g house of bread

a man^e went out^f from Bethlehem^g of Judah^h

^h confession

to exile in the country of the Moabites, with

ⁱ the Church *[handwritten:] g. moves through the world*

his wifeⁱ and two sons. And he was called

[handwritten:] with his wife, the Church

Elimelech, and his wife was Naomi, and

^j prophets and apostles

two sons, one Maalon, the other Chilion,^j

^k or from Ephrath, the wife of Caleb.

Ephrathites^k of Bethlehem of Judah. And

^l Judah, which follows the Law^m badly.

having come to the country of the Moabites^l,

^m and he did not stay, but waited there on the cross

they stayed there. And Elimelech, Naomi's

ⁿ the Church ^o in the exile of this world

husband, died, and sheⁿ was left^o with her

^p learned men

sons.^p They took Moabite wives, one of

^q her neck

whom was called Orpha,^q and the other

Ruth. And so they continued there for ten

^r prophets and apostles

years, and both^r died, that is, Maalon and

^s the Church

Chilion; and the woman^s was left, deprived

is the Church, is beautiful, as when it says, *You are beautiful my love* [1201A; Song 4:1].

Died] After the completion of devout labour, they passed from the exile of this world to the heavenly kingdom; so that, having fulfilled the ten commandments, they received the ten beatitudes [1202C].

And the woman was left] after the Lord's ascension, on this pilgrimage, in the exile of this world [1202C].

[handwritten:] prophets predicting Christ

Maalon] "From a window," or "from the beginning." This is the chorus of prophets through whom the first light of faith proceeds, as if through a window, who were indeed the first preachers of the true light, that is, of Christ [1201A-B].

They took Moabite wives] Because the apostles associated with two peoples, namely the Jews and the Gentiles [1201D].

[left column glosses:]

[handwritten:] Jewish coll. of homiletic commentaries

There was a famine] There was a famine of the word of God because of the scarcity of men learned in spiritual things (to whom the authority to judge is given), for even the Law was corrupted by Jewish traditions (PL 108:1199D; cf. Amos 8:11).

A man went etc.] Namely, Christ, born in Bethlehem in Judah, who made the pilgrimage of this world with his wife, that is, the Church, and with his two sons, namely, the two orders of prophets and apostles, who were freed from the slavery of sin by the blood of Christ [1200D].

[handwritten:] a diff family of readings

A man went] whom some interpret as the ten commandments, and his wife as the Synagogue, and the two sons as kingly and priestly honor, who arranged marriage-bonds for themselves, not only among the people of the Jews but also among outsiders, just as it was in the time of David and Solomon and the other kings [1200C].

Two sons] You might be freed¹ by the blood of Christ, from kingly and priestly honor to the order of prophets and apostles.

In the country of Moab] namely in the country of the devil, who is the prince of this world.

Elimelech] "my God is king." This is Christ, to whom it is said, *Listen to the voice of my prayer, my king and my God* [1201A; Ps. 5:2].

Naomi] That is, "beautiful": *You are beautiful, my love* etc. [Song 4:1]; "beautiful or a comfort." Naomi, that

---

[right column glosses:]

Chilion] "Fulfilment." *[handwritten:] fulfils the prophecies → full understanding* These are the apostles who have brought the enigmas of the prophets out into the fulfilment of full understanding. These were born, deservedly, Ephrathites of Bethlehem in Judah who, filled with heavenly bread themselves, gathered the fruits of preaching by preaching the Gospel. For "Ephrathite" means someone bearing fruit, "Bethlehem" means house of bread, and "Judah" confession. Whence, *Give them these things to eat* (Mark 6:37; Lk. 9:13; Matt. 14:16). Again, *Go out and preach the Gospel of the kingdom of God* (Mark 16:15). And elsewhere, *I chose you from the world that you should go and bear fruit* [1201B; John 15:16].

They took Moabite wives] These are the faithful people from amongst the Jews, who were the first to understand the stronghold of faith and the strength of religious service [1202A]. Ruth] "Seeing," or "hurrying," or "ceasing."² In her is designated the obedience and trust of the Gentiles, of whom it is said, *People whom I had not known, served me* etc. [Ps. 18:43]. And elsewhere, *Ethiopia hurried to give a hand to God* [Ps. 68:31]. Therefore two peoples, of faith and of the chosen of God, will be called to marriage by holy preachers, so that one sheepfold may come from a diverse flock [John 10].

Two sons] Prophets and apostles, whose bodily presence she was deprived of [1202D].

And she arose] The Church pays her debts conscientiously, so that the people whom the apostles and prophets taught might be led in their time to the unity of faith and the society of the Christian religion, which Scripture refers to, teaching that the just man is not abandoned, *neither shall his seed seek bread* [Ps. 36: 25] which comes down from heaven [1202D].

Go home] The Church does not act indiscriminately, nor accept anyone indiscriminately. Whence, *Do not believe every spirit, but test whether the spirits are of God* [1 John 4:1]. Those whom the Synagogue sends back from coming to the faith of Christ fall in with her wishes, and rightly, for she knows herself to be weak and exhausted, overcome by truth, saying, *Turn back, my daughters* [1203B–D].

Turn back] The voice of the Synagogue who, having been forsaken by a man (that is, David) and bereaved of her sons (that is, of kings and princes), admits the truth, does not keep silent about her overwhelming fault, and confesses to God that she is weak and barren in conceiving children after the advent of Christ [1203D].

of her two sons and her husband.

And she arose in order to start for her native

land from the Moabite country, with both

ᵗnamely, the people

her daughters-in-law;ᵗ for she had heard that

the Lord had looked after his own people

ᵘof Life

and had given them food.ᵘ Therefore she set

ᵛthis world

out from the place of her exileᵛ with both

ʷthe people

daughters-in-law,ʷ and when they were

already on the road which would take them

ˣto Christ or his commandments ʸsteadfastly

backˣ to the land of Judah,ʸ she said to them,

"Go home to your mothers; may the Lord

have mercy on you, just as you had mercy

on my dead family, and on me. May the

Lord grant that you find rest in the houses

of men that you choose." And she kissed

them. And, raising their voices, they began

to weep and said, "We will go with you to

your people." She answered them, "Go back,

ᶻelsewhere, to the Moabites

my daughters.ᶻ Why come with me? Do I

ᵃbelievers in Christ

have more sons in my wombᵃ that you may

ᵇforsaken by Christ

hope for husbands from me?ᵇ Turn back, my

Orpha] "Believers" are signified by these women (one of whom, grieving and mourning, leaves her mother-in-law; the other, of determined spirit, stays), some of whom (signifed by Orpha who turned back to her gods) after receiving the grace of baptism, will fall back from the fellowship of faith to original errors; others, however, of immutable purpose, (signified by Ruth) follow through the grace which has been received [1204A–B].

Orpha] "Believers" are signified by these women (one of whom, grieving and mourning, leaves her mother-in-law; the other, of determined spirit, stays), some of whom (signifed by Orpha who turned back to her gods) after receiving the grace of baptism, will fall back from the fellowship of faith to original errors; others, however, of immutable purpose, (signified by Ruth) follow through the grace which has been received [1204A–B].

Wherever you go] Thus the Church, having been called from the Gentiles, abandoned her native land, which is idolatry, gave up carnal longings, declared her God to be that God in whom the saints believed and that she would go where the flesh of Christ ascended, and for whose name she would suffer in this world until death, and (unite) with the people of the saints and patriarchs and prophets; whence, *Rejoice, you nations, with his people* [1204B–C paraphrasing Isidore; Deut. 32:43; Rom. 15:10].

c to the observance of the Law

daughters,c and leave me, for I am already

an old woman, not suited to the bonds of

marriage; even if I were able to conceive

this very night and bear sons, if you wished

to wait for them until they grew up and

completed the years of puberty, you would

be old women before you were married. I

pray you not to stay, my daughters, because

your difficulty oppresses me more than it

d vengeance; a grave affliction or punishment

does you, and the hand of the Lordd is

turned against me." And raising their voices,

again they began to cry. Orpha kissed her

e to the error of idolatry

mother-in-law and turned back;e Ruth stuck

f the faith of the Church

by her mother-in-law.f Naomi said to her,

"Look! Your sister has gone back to her

people and to her gods: go with her." She

answered, "Do not oppose me to make me

leave you and go away. I shall go wherever

you go; I shall stay wherever you stay.

g through merits, aided by grace alone, by free vocation

Your people are my people,g and your God

is my God. Whatever earth receives you

when you die, I shall die there and I shall be

Therefore, seeing] The Gentile people, having stubborn hearts, followed preachers into the holy land, and into Bethlehem, the city of God where it [the people] might prepare to receive a spouse, born of the lineage of Abraham, in whom all nations of the earth might be blessed [1204D].

Call me not] The Synagogue recognizes the ruin which she justly suffers after the advent of Christ, and refuses to be called beautiful, because she sees the era of her prosperity is over [1205A].

buried there. May the Lord do these things for me, and let him add things, if even death [h] because nothing except death can do so separates me and you."[h] Therefore, seeing that Ruth had made up her mind and had decided to go with her, Naomi was not willing to resist her nor to persuade her to return to her own people; and they went on together and came to Bethlehem. When they had entered the town, knowledge of them spread swiftly to all, and the women said, "This is Naomi herself." But she answered, "Call me not Naomi (that is, beautiful), but call me Mara (that is, bitterness) because the Almighty has filled me greatly with bitterness. I set out full and the Lord has led me back empty. Why then call me Naomi, whom the Lord has brought low and the Almighty has afflicted?" Thus Naomi came with Ruth, the Moabite woman, her daughter-in-law, from the land of her exile; and she came back into Bethlehem when the first barley was being harvested.

Naomi] This signifies that the Church, when pressed by tribulation, should not love delight but should seek future glory. Whence, *I am black but beautiful, O daughters of Jerusalem* [1204D–5A; Song 1:5].

When the first barley] That is, when the Law of Christ's incarnation transformed the order to the mystery of his passion.[3] For the barley harvest is threshed out at the time of the passion of the Lord, which happens during the month of new things, that is, the first month. Therefore it was well that they went to Bethlehem at this time, when the Law (which teaches that Christ was born in Bethlehem), foretells His death at Passover (that is, in the month of new things). Holy Church also works as hard as she can so that she might imbue those whom He calls to faith with the incarnation, passion, [and] resurrection. Or the barley harvest means the faith of those Jews who, having carried out the sacramental act of the passion, first came to faith through the preaching of the apostles, and who elsewhere gathered five loaves of barley bread for the Lord [1205B–C; John 6].

Notes

1. The Latin has a possible double meaning here, since *liberi* suggests both "free" and "children," referring back to the two sons.

2. This is made clear by Rabanus' expansions, which are not in the Gloss: she "sees" faith, and "hurries" to it, and "ceases" to be pagan.

3. Rabanus Maurus reads somewhat differently, though the expression is still rather roundabout: "When the Law turns from teaching the people the order of their own story to the mystery of Christ's incarnation." Both refer to the change from the Old to the New covenant.

There was a kinsman of Elimelech] This man [who] was kin to Elimelech, is Christ, the lamb of the Law and the legislator, for he had been promised by the Law, and was born in flesh from the patriarchs and from the Jewish nation. Whence, *The Lord your God will raise up for you, from among your brothers, a prophet, as I am, and you shall hear him* [cf. Deut. 18:15]. He is the powerful one who will end the power of the princes of this world and subjugate the whole earth to his command, and [he will end the power] of great riches because he is the possessor of the heavens and the earth, and in him are all treasures of wisdom and knowledge and *For he himself is virtue and wisdom (of God)* [1205D–6A; Col. 2:3].

Go to a field etc. This field is the knowledge of heavenly study. The harvest is spiritual discernment. The harvesters are preachers. The remaining ears of corn are the opinions of the Scriptures which, by the mystery of concealment, are very often left behind for the exercise of contemplation, like fuller, deeper senses.[1] The Gentile people, therefore, ardently desire the Church's learning, so that they might be admitted to the contemplation of divine Law and the fellowship of the saints, and they might be refreshed by the lessons and examples of the saints [1206B–C].

CHAPTER 2

But there was a kinsman of the man

Elimelech, a man of power and of great

wealth, Boaz by name. Ruth, the Moabite

woman, said to her mother-in-law, "If you

ᵃ the Church

agree, I will go into a field[a] and

collect the gleanings which have

escaped the hands of the reapers,

wherever I meet with kindness from a

merciful landowner." She answered

her, "Go, my daughter; go, indeed, and

collect the grain behind the backs of

the reapers." It happened, however,

that the field was owned by Boaz,

ᵇ that is, of the Law

who was a kinsman of Elimelech.[b] And

behold, he came from Bethlehem, and

he said to the reapers, "The Lord be

ᶜ the words of salvation

with you."[c] They answered him, "May

the Lord bless you." And Boaz said to

the young man who was in charge of

And Boaz said] Because Christ questioned one of the learned men who commanded the lesser priests when He challenged him to preach, as though [He were] ignorant about the faith of the people [1207A; Matt. 21:23 et seq.; Matt. 22:45 et seq.].

Boaz] means "the fortitude of God." Whence, *And his name shall be called, wonderful, counsellor, God, strong, father of all ages* [Isai. 9:6].

Reapers] The saints are the harvest who are gathered and laid down in the granary of God, the harvesters are angels [1206B; Matt. 13:39].

Gleanings] The ears of corn signify the faithful remnant who, when the rest have been transported to heaven, are left with us as an example [1206B].

It happened etc. Because holy Church belongs to Christ, whose spouse and body she is. Of whom it is said, *The Lord is my strength and my song* (Ps. 117:14); and elsewhere, *The Lord is strong and powerful in battle* (Ps. 24:8). He is the kinsman of Elimelech, who was born in Bethlehem and from the house of David, having the witness of the Law and the prophets. He, at whose birth angels sang, *Glory to God in the highest, and peace to men of goodwill on earth* (Lk. 2:14) brought words of salvation (and peace) to His family; at His coming in Jerusalem, the crowd along the way shouted, saying, *Blessed is He who comes in the name of the Lord* [1206C–D; Matt. 21:9]. And he said] Because holy Church perseveres in the field of divine reading after the harvesters (that is, after the preachers who gather in the mysteries of the Scriptures), so that she stores away in the hiding place of her mind the witness and example of the virtuous [1207B].

the reapers, "Who does this girl belong to?"

He answered, "she is a Moabite woman who

came with Naomi from the country of the

Moabites, and she asked if she might collect

the leftover grain, following in the footsteps

of the harvesters; and from early this

^d from the beginning of faith to the completion of good works

morning^d till now she has stood in the

^e to old superstition

field, and not gone home^e, even for a

moment." And Boaz said to Ruth,

"Hear me, daughter. Do not go to

another field to collect the grain,

nor leave here: but join my young

girls, and where they reap the grain,

follow them. For I have given orders

to my young men that no-one should

bother you: and if you are thirsty, go

to my baggage and drink the water

which the young people drink." And

she, falling on her face on the

ground and revering him, said to him,

"Why have I found favor in your

sight, that you should think me, a

Do not go to another field]
Meaning, "do not leave the state of faith, lest you follow the errors of the heretics or schismatics," but rather join with the minds of the saints, so that you fear the holy Scriptures, meditating on them, and fulfilling them by deeds. And having drunk divine wisdom from the books of the two Testaments, from which the young people (that is to say, the saints), drink, you may drink of it too [1207C–D].

Do not go] meaning, "do not leave either the teachings of the saints or the refreshment of their examples."

And she, falling on her face] The Church gives thanks to the Savior of the Gentiles, who has deemed her worthy to be cared for. He answers her, "Be pleased with yourself." For by the death of her husband (that is, the devil), she left idolatrous parents, and the land of her birth (that is, carnal desire), and took up fellowship with the saints, who were unknown to her before this, since she followed the lusts of the "old Adam" [1207D–8A].

She, falling] Ezechiel, seeing the glory of the Lord, fell on his face and adored him.

Why have I found favor etc. Note the humility of the Gentile church, which knows herself to be unequal to so much grace, nor dares to compare herself to the primitive church; whence she says, *For I am not worthy so much as to gather up the crumbs...* (Matt. 15:27; Luke 16:21; Mark 7:28). And elsewhere, *O Lord, I am not worthy to come in under your roof but only speak the word* etc. [1208B–C; Matt. 8:8; Luke 7:6].

Reward] Eternal glory, whence, *Seek and you shall find, so that your joy may be complete* [1208A; John 16:24].

Wings] the two testaments by which God protects those who flee to him. Whence, *I will hope in the shadow of your wings, until I might cross over* [1208B; Ps. 56:2] (until iniquity passes away).

For her price is far above rubies (Prov. 31:10)

foreign woman,ᶠ worthy?" He answered her, "Everything has been reported to me: what you did for your mother-in--law after the death of her husband, and that you abandoned your parents and the land where you were born

ᵍ I have not found such faith in Israel (Mt. 8:10; Lk. 7:9)

and came to this peopleᵍ which you did

ʰ People whom I had not known served me (Ps. 18:43)

not previously know.ʰ·ⁱ The Lord repays

ⁱ Since I have not known my servant (Ps. 17:45)

you for your deeds, and you shall receive full reward from the Lord God of Israel, to whom you came, and under whose wings you flew." And she said, "I have found favor in your sight my Lord, who has comforted me, and who has spoken to the heart of your handmaiden, as though I were like one of your girls, which I am not." And Boaz said to her, "When it is evening, come here and eat the bread and dip your morsel in the vinegar." And so she sat beside the reapers and he collected barley-flour for her, and

Your deeds] your faith. Hence, *This is the work of God, that you believe in Him whom He sent* (Jn 6:29; 1208A).

When it is evening] It was at mealtime that He said to his disciples, *Go, and teach all the people, baptizing them in the name of the Father and the Son and the Holy Spirit* (Matt. 28:19). And before that He said to them, *Do not go to the ways of the Gentiles* [1208C; Matt. 10:5].

Dip your morsel] Namely, into the Law which, having been practiced for a long time and persisted in by the first people, completely lost its native flavor which was corrupted by the seasonings (and traditions) of the Pharisees. The Church dips her morsel (that is, the mystery of the incarnation of Christ), into this, she learns that it [the incarnation] was [taught] in the Old Testament, and so she believes more firmly, because she grasps what was prefigured, long ago [1208D].

In the vinegar] Meaning the Gentile Church joined herself to the holy preachers through faith [1208D–9A].

She ate] Because she refreshed her faithful mind by knowledge of divine Law [1209A].

And was satisfied etc] Because she considered deeply each word she heard [1209A].

Took the rest away] Because she retained the words in her heart, and worked so that she might understand more by concentrated meditation [1209A].

Commanded etc.] Note the humility of the landowner, who not only allowed her to collect the leftover ears of the Testaments, but even commands her to have sheaves of knowledge from his largesse [1209A–B].

She may glean] Because He does not despise the weakness of the Gentile people, nor dwell on early errors, but guides them with sagacity to the capability of knowledge [1209B].

With a rod] Because holy Church draws out the spiritual sense from the letter of the Law with the rod of discernment [1209C].

About an ephah] This reading teaches the catholic faith by the confession of the Holy Trinity via the standard [size] of an ephah, which contains three measures. This signifies one substance in divinity, and three persons in selfhood [1209C].

she ate and was satisfied and took the rest away. And from then on it became the custom for her to collect the grain. Indeed, Boaz commanded his boys, saying, "Even should she wish to reap with you, do not prevent her, and even throw out grain from your bundles on purpose and leave it there, so that she may glean without shame; and no-one should reprove her for gleaning." Accordingly, she collected grain in the field until the evening, and cutting and shaking out what she had collected with a rod, she found it was an ephah's worth of barley, that is, three measures. Carrying this, she went back to the city and showed her mother-in-law; on top of this she brought out and gave her the rest of her meal, so that she was made full.[3]

And her mother-in-law said to her,

Carrying this] For she shows her faith in mother Church. Or [it means], the Church shows to the Synagogue that grace which she received by the gift of her spouse, and she shows it to her mother, the Synagogue, so that it might challenge her to believe [1209C–D].

Gave her] namely, from the fullness of his heart, the food of preaching, *You with your own hand drove out the nations, but them you planted* (Ps. 44:2).

"Where did you glean today, and where did you do this work? May he who was merciful to you be blessed." And she told her about how she had been treated, and said the man's name, that he was called Boaz. And Naomi replied, "May he be blessed by the Lord, since he has performed a [k] to the Gentiles [people] who were buried in sin service for the dead[k] with the same kindness which he has shown to the living." And again she said, "Our [l] Christ neighbor is a true man."[l] And Ruth said, "He ordered me to join in with his reapers until all the fields were reaped." Her mother-in-law said to her, "My daughter, it is better for [m] with holy souls you to go out to reap with his girls,[m] in case someone stops you gleaning in another field." And so she joined herself to Boaz's girls, and reaped with them until the barley and wheat were stored in the granaries.

He also ordered] Because Christ commands everyone to come to Him, so that they may be yoked rather with His faithful believers at the harvest of the spiritual crop than with strangers, her [Ruth's] mother-in-law gives in to her persuasion, saying, *My daughter, it is better* etc., for Synagogue is not able to deny that this is good and useful [1210C].

Another field] namely, the doctrine of heretics or schismatics, where there are quarrels and disputes [1210D].

Until the barley harvest etc.] This means, for as long as she stays with learned men, meditating on the Scriptures, until she can store away knowledge of the Old and New Testaments in the storeroom of her heart, to have enough food for her soul [1211A].

Barley] the letter of the Law which was given as food to the Jews as [barley is] to beasts of burden [1210D].

Wheat] means the grace of the New Testament which was gathered for food for reasonable[2] people, in which the body and blood of Christ is offered. From which it is said, *Unless a grain of wheat falls into the ground and dies, it alone remains* [1210D; John 12: 24–25].

Neighbor] Mother Church, gathered together by the gracious kindness shown to the Gentile people, recognized her neighbor and, having heard the name, she recalled past kindness, whence, *I was mindful of ancient days and I meditated on all your works* (Ps. 142:5). The Synagogue knows the goodness of the Gentiles, the power of the Lord, and the strength of her protector, through the preaching of the Church; and at length, having grasped the truth, she blesses the name of the Lord who held to His kindness towards the dead as much as He offered it to the living [1210A–B] (to the Jews, since they enjoy those kindnesses through the understanding of the life-giving Law).

Neighbor] to the Synagogue according to the flesh, to the Church according to the union of spirit [1210C].

Man] the spirit gives life, through the understanding of the Law.

Notes

1. *Plenior* in Gloss, but *planior*, "clearer," in Rabanus.

2. "rationibus"; ? receptive.

3. This refers back to—and reverses—Naomi's statement to the women, in chapter 1: "I set out full and the Lord has led me back empty."

I will try to get you rest]
The primitive [Church]
takes thought for the
Gentile [Church] to make
her the bride of Christ
[1211B].

Threshing floor] Christ
winnows this Synagogue of
the Jews (where the barley
of the Law was stored)
when, preaching the gospel
in Judah, he threshed the
plans and wills each one
held in respect of himself.
Whence, *But Jesus would
not entrust himself to them,
because he knew all people
and needed no one to testify
about anyone; for he
himself knew what was in
everyone* [1211B; John 2:
24–25].

Threshing floor] For here
Christ is encountered and
calls the human race back to
Himself [1211C].

That he might not see you
etc.] Because the faith of the
Gentile church did not appear before Christ had fulfilled the mystery of the incarnation. Living corpore-
ally amongst people, He ate
and drank; and finally,
feasting with His disciples,
He imparted the sacraments
of His body and blood to
them. However, when the
mystery of the Christ's
overlordship had been fulfilled, the Church faithfully
came to the faith from the
Gentiles [1211D].

Goes to sleep] that is, goes
to die for us, so that he
achieved all things.
Whence, *If I am lifted up
from the earth, I will draw
all men to me* [1212A; John
12:32].

CHAPTER 3

When, however, she returned to her mother-
in-law, she was told by her, "My daughter,
I will try to get you rest and provide for
your welfare. This Boaz, whose girls you
joined in the field, is our relative, and
tonight he winnows the grain on the
[a] with the water of baptism or the tears of penitence
threshing floor of the granary. Wash[a]
[b] with chrism or with the oil of the Holy Spirit
yourself, therefore, and anoint[b] yourself, and
[c] the embellishments of virtue
put on your best clothes[c] and go down to the
threshing floor. The man may not see you
until he has finished eating and drinking.
But when he leaves to go to sleep, take note
of the place where he sleeps, and go and
turn back that part of the blanket covering
his feet, and slip yourself underneath, and
lie there. He will tell you what you should
do."[1] And she answered, "I will do whatever
you order."

And she went down to the threshing floor,
and did all that her mother-in-law had

Place] of the suffering and,
of course, of death
[1212A].

Turn back etc.] As if to say,
"Understand that Christ
died for you; come with a
devout mind; scatter the
cloaking letter of the Old
Testament in which the
sacrament of the incarna-
tion of Christ is covered;
and when you have known
the salvation promised you,
humbly take refuge in His
help so that you might remain there for all time"
[1212A].

The man may not] Because
it is necessary that you
learn the order of your salvation for yourself. If,
however, you ascribe the
words of Naomi to Syna-
gogue, you will discover in
the Law and the prophets
that she will come to faith
after the passion, because
of the Church of the
Gentiles [1212B].

I will do whatever you
order] The obedience of the
Church deserves the fulfilment of her desire.
Whence, *Woman, great is
your faith. Let it be as you
wish* [1212D; Matt. 15:28].

Boaz had eaten and drunk] Christ ate and drank when He gave the sacraments to the apostles in the meal of His body and blood. Whence, *Because the children are partakers of the body and blood, and He Himself has been a partaker of them* [1212D; Hebr. 2:14].

Pile of hay] The witness of the Scriptures. Whence, *The son of man goes, as it was written* (Matt. 26:24). Or else it means, next to the crowds of faithful souls whom He called back from the inferno by His death. The Church hastens to this bed and turns back the cover [1213A–B].

In the middle of the night] This is said because it shows the swift faith of the Church, which we should imitate when the darkness of errors envelop the world [1213B].

Spread your blanket] The Church desires the grace of faith and of the protection of Christ before all things.

Your blanket] She who sought to have a cover spread over herself deserved to receive a blessing; for whoever fully receives the grace of faith, will possess blessing and virtue equally [1213C–D].

Former pity] Because, taking thought for yourself, you have abandoned idolatry [1213D].

Latest pity] Because after you came to Christ you persevered with constancy in the faith [1213D].

ordered her. And when Boaz had eaten and drunk and had made merry, and had left to go to sleep next to the pile of hay, she came secretly and turned back the blanket covering his feet and slipped herself underneath it. And behold, in the middle of the night, the man was afraid and was

d the Church

perturbed: and he saw the womand lying at

e humbly venerating the sacrament of the incarnation

his feete and said to her, "Who are you?"f

f Christ sought the confession of the Church

And she answered, "I am Ruth, your handmaid. Spread your blanket over your servant, because you are her kinsman." And he said, "Daughter, you are blessed by the Lord, and you have surpassed your former pity with your latest pity, because you have not run after young men, poor or rich. Do not be afraid, therefore; but what you have asked me, I shall do for you. For everyone who lives within the gates of my city knows you to be a woman of virtue. I do not deny that you are my relative; but there is someone who is a closer relative to you than

You did not run after young men] Heretics and schismatics who do not have mature counsel, because they are always unstable and uncertain [1213D].

Whatever you say . . .] *Ask and you shall receive* (John 16:24), *Seek and you shall find* (Matt. 7:7). The kindness of Christ will grant whatever you ask for in faith [1214A].

Everyone knows] Because it was the conviction of the faithful that the Church is full of virtue, of which it is said, *Whoever finds a strong woman* [1214B; Prov. 31:10].

Someone who is a closer relative] This refers to John the Baptist, who was thought to be Christ, but who did not usurp the name of spouse but, rather, guarded it for Christ, saying, *Whoever has the bride is the bridegroom* (John 3:29). He is the closer relative because he was born first in the world. It also means that he is near to the ten commandments of the Law, which seemed nearer to Synagogue than to the Church, because the commandments were given specially to the people and were prior in time [than grace] [1214C–D].

And so she slept at his feet]
Because she waited patient-
ly, resting in the hope of the
incarnation, until the darkness of unfaithfulness departed [1214D].

She arose before men knew
each other] Because, before
the Jews had been imbued
with the teaching of the
Law, they had grasped the
rules of its nature. The
Gentile Church arose,
shaking off the sleep of
idleness, being born into the
dawn of faith, and hastened
to the grace of Christ
[1214D–15A].

Take care in case anyone
know] Lest you seek human
praise from your conversation, *When you give alms,
let your left hand not know
what your right hand is
doing* [1215A; Matt. 6:3].

me. Stay here tonight, and in the morning,

if he wishes to preserve the law of

propinquity,² all well and good; but if he

does not wish it, I will receive you into my

household without any hesitation, as the

Lord lives. Sleep until morning."

And so she slept at his feet till daylight.

And she arose before men knew each other,

and Boaz said, "Take care, in case anyone

knows that you came here." And again he
^g expand your faith
said, "Stretch out the blanket^g which covers
^h cultivate the works which you hold in your heart
you and hold it in both hands."^h As she held

it outstretched he measured out six measures

of barley and placed it on the blanket.

Carrying this, she went into the city and
^i the primitive Church or the Synagogue
went to her mother-in-law,^i who said to her,

"What did you do, daughter?" And she told

her everything that the man had done for

her. And she said, "Behold, he gave me six

measures of barley, and he said, 'I do not

want you to return to your mother-in-law

He measured out six
measures] Because the
manner of perfect action is
given to her along with a
capacity for understanding,
so that she might be dedi-
cated, inside and out, to
divine service. The number
six can also signify this:
that the Lord, in the sixth
age,⁴ gave the barley of the
Law—spiritually under-
stood—to the Gentile
Church [1215C].

Carrying this] Namely,
having been enriched by
the gifts of Christ, and having been loaded up with the
fruits of virtues [1215D].

Everything that the man
had done for her] Namely,
the exploits of God, so that
the primitive Church might
be challenged to praise, or
the Synagogue to conver-
sion [1215D].

For the man will not rest]
The Church promises faithfully that Truth will not
cease to fulfill the promise
which says, *Whoever be-
lieved and was baptized will
be saved* [1215D–16A;
Mark 16:16].

empty[-handed]'."[3] And Naomi said, "Just wait, daughter, and see what the outcome will be. For the man will not rest until he has done what he said."

For the man will not rest]
Because Christ takes the
prophecy which was writ-
ten about His incarnation to
its fulfillment.

Notes

1. The somewhat ambiguous sense of what is actually going to happen here is undoubtedly intended by the author. He heightens the tension in the passage by using a number of Hebrew sexual euphemisms, most notably "feet," which could also mean "genitals." The anxiety is meant not to titillate the reader but to show how Ruth and Boaz *might* have behaved had they not chosen the virtuous route. For further discussion, see *Ruth*, trans. E. F. Campbell, Jr., *The Anchor Bible*, vol. 7 (Garden City, N.Y.: Doubleday & Company, Inc., 1975), pp. 121, 130–32.

2. The law of propinquity, or of the closer relation, refers to the institution of "levirate marriage" described in Deut. 25:5–10. If a woman were widowed, without a male heir, it was her husband's closest relative's duty to marry her and conceive a son, who would both carry on his father's name and provide for his mother. See further T. Thompson and D. Thompson, "Some Legal Problems in the Book of Ruth," *Vetus Testamentum* 18 (1968), pp. 79–99.

3. Note once again the references to empty and full in chaps 1 and 2. Ruth goes to Boaz empty but he sends her back to Naomi full. Later, she will be "full" with his child.

4. From the patristic era on, the history of Creation had been divided into six ages, matching the six days on which God created the world. The ages were: Adam to Noah; Noah to Abraham; Abraham to David; David to the Babylonian captivity; the captivity to Jesus; and Jesus to the end of the world. Each of the ages was thought to be about 1000 years long. A. Luneau, *L'histoire du salut chez les Pères de l'Église: la doctrine des âges du monde* (Paris, 1964).

Then Boaz went up to the gate] Because He took up the flesh in which He appeared, in the virgin's womb. About this door it is said, *This door will be shut and may not be opened, and no man will go through it, because the Lord, the God of Israel has gone in through it* [1216A–B; Ezek. 44:2].

Pause a little] Because Christ saw the Law had been established for the Jews in their time, and He ordered it to submit to him, because He directed it to give witness to the mystery of His overlordship. In another way, He sees the kinsman "pass by" at the coming of His precursor whom, after the fashion of human life, He saw hurrying past, and He turned, in compassion, to the office of herald [calling him by name; 1216C].

Ten men] The Fathers of the Old Testament, who kept the decalogue of the Law and knew that it presaged the incarnation of Christ [1216D].

CHAPTER 4

Boaz went up to the town gate and sat there.

And when he saw his relative (whom he had

spoken of earlier), go past, he said to him,
[a] through Gabriel saying, *His name will be called John* (Jn 1:6)
calling him by his name, [a] "Pause a little

while, and sit here." And he paused and sat
[b] in witness of His coming
down. Then Boaz, bringing over[b] ten men

from amongst the town elders, said to them,

"sit down here." And when they were

settled, he said to his neighbor, "Naomi,

who returned from the country of the

Moabites, is selling part of the field

belonging to our brother Elimelech. I

wished you to hear this and to tell you this

in front of the whole seated assembly and

elders of my people. If you wish to have the

field, buy it and have it, by the law of

propinquity. However, if you do not want it,

tell me, so I know what I should do. For

there is no nearer relative than you who

have priority, and I who am second."

Whereupon he replied, "I will buy the field."

Part of the field] He offered the lawyers a part of Naomi's land to buy. This refers to that part of the people which was left behind after grace had appeared; and He showed it to the masters of the Synagogue as a remedy, so that they should know their sickness and, because they could not heal themselves, they might trust themselves to a true doctor, as was said to the lepers, *Go, show yourselves to the priests* (Luke 17:14), and when they went they were made clean [1216D–17A].

The land had to stay in one family by Jewish law — gift of God

To keep alive] This signifies no other possession of the people (as if it were a part of a field) than the marriage of the Church with Christ,[1] which revived the ancient name "sons of God," that the saints had had from the beginning: *Sons of God, seeing the daughters of men* etc. (Gen. 6:2), and Luke says Adam was the son of God (Luke 3:38). It revived in the Church of the Gentiles through the grace of God, whence, *He gave them power to become the sons of God* (John 1:12). The decalogue of the Law was not able to revive this name among the nations. If, however, you refer this to John the Baptist, you will find him yielding to the authority of his kinsman, and saying, *I baptize with water. Among you stands one whom you do not know, the one who is coming after me. I am not worthy to untie the thong of his sandal* (John 1:26–27). And elsewhere, *I am not the Messiah, but I have been sent ahead of him. He who has the bride is the bridegroom* (John 3: 28–29). Thus the Law gives way to the Gospel, *For the Law entered so that wrongs might abound. But where wrongs abounded, grace abounded so much more* (Rom. 5:20). Indeed, reproof was made to the previous covenant on account of its weakness. Rather, the introduction of a better hope, through which we are made neighbor to God, was made through Jesus Christ [1217B–18B].

To which Boaz said, "When you buy the field from the woman's hand, you must also take on Ruth, the Moabite woman whose husband is dead, to keep alive the name[5] of your relative in your heredity." To which he replied, "I cede my right by the law of propinquity; for I should not harm the future of my family. You may have my privilege, which I declare that I give up freely." Now this, indeed, was the ancient custom in Israel amongst kinsmen, that whenever anyone ceded his right under the law to another, so that it was conceded definitely, the man undid his own sandal and gave it to his neighbor.[6] In Israel, this was proof of the giving up of the right. Boaz therefore said to his neighbor, "Take off your sandal." And he immediately undid his sandal. And he said, before the elders and all the people, "You are witnesses today that I will take over all the things which belonged to Elimelech and Chilion and

Now this was the custom] The sandal is a veil of mysteries. The Old Law released the sandal from his foot, and gave it to Christ, because it could not show the sacraments to the magistrates of the people, but reserved this for Christ to do. John, therefore, did not claim the sandal for himself but for Christ, because he understood Christ alone to be fit for the bride, whence he says, *I am not worthy to loose the thong of his sandal* [1218B–C; Luke 3:16].

You are witnesses] And so Christ has sufficient witnesses from each Testament because He Himself fertilizes (with the seed of the Word of God) the Gentile people, whom the ten commandments—now spiritually at an end—cannot fertilize; so that they possess all things that the saints, both those coming before and those coming after, possessed [1219B].

Before the elders] Isidore: The blessing shown ten of the elders that all nations are blessed in the name of Jesus Christ. For to the Greeks, iota, which is the first letter of the name "Jesus," signifies ten [1219B–C].

May your house] They prayed for the prosperity of the Church of the Gentiles, that she might receive the grace of fertility, which the first parents of the Israelites had had [1219D].

Rachel] "hope of eternal contemplation" (or "a type of internal contemplation"), having certain (or "inward") understanding of truth. Rachel herself *of good and beautiful face* (Gen. 39:6,17), who loved anyone who loved piety, was on account of this kept back by Laban (which means whitewash: *though your sins were scarlet, they will be as white as snow* [Isai. 1:18]), who compared her to the grace of God (Gen. 29) [1220A].

Leah] Without faith, the trial of this life we live is laborious and uncertain when it comes to making provision for those we wish to care for. Leah herself, who was said to be weak of eye,[2] was the first wife of Jacob [1220A].

Perez] who possessed the grace[3] of the Gentile people, because in birth order he preceeded his brother, who stuck out his hand first (Gen. 38); for Israel first stuck out her hand in the work of the Law and the prophets, and then drew it back, stained with the blood of Christ himself. But afterwards, the Gentile people sprang forth, so that *the first shall be last and the last shall be first* (Matt. 20:16).

Maalon, handed down to Naomi; and Ruth, the Moabite woman, the wife of Maalon, I will take in marriage, and I will revive the name of the dead in her children, so that his name of his [Elimelech's] family and brothers will not be lost amongst the people. I call you as witnesses of this act." All the people who were at the gate and the elders answered, "We are witnesses; the Lord made this woman, who has come into your house, like Rachel and Leah, who built the house of Israel, so that she may be an example of virtue in Ephrathah, and she may have a name famous throughout Bethlehem. And may your house be [established] from the seed which the Lord will have given to you from this girl, as was the house of Perez, whom Tamar bore of Judah."

And so Boaz took Ruth and made her his wife; and he went in to her and the Lord

Tamar] also means "changing" or "bitterness." For the Gentile Church changed both her name and her character; for what was foul and bitter in idolatry became sweet and beautiful in penitence [1220B–C].

The Lord will have given to you] Because Christ, in union with the Church, begets spiritual children, whence, *The barren bore many children and she who already had many sons was made weak* [1221A; 1 Sam. 2:5].

Blessed be the Lord] The Church is always being fertilized by the gifts of the holy Spirit. And when some have departed to perpetual light, others take their place, so that the name of Christians endures forever, and the most holy Mother [Church] has the consolation of new offspring in her old age. So when the patriarchs and prophets have departed, the apostles and evangelists follow on, whence, *Children have been born to you in place of your fathers* [1221B; Ps. 45:17].

For from your daughter-in-law] The daughter-in-law of Synagogue is the Gentile Church, who was married to Christ, born from the Synagogue [1221C].
+ born] the Christian people.

You had seven sons] Namely, a multitude of those who were nourished in the doctrine of Law by the Old Testament; and who, of course, did not believe the word of the Lord, and sacrificed their sons and daughters to demons; and who, in the end, killed Christ and persecuted his apostles [1221D–1222A].

And Naomi took the child] That is, she carried him whom she was not able to give birth to with the Law, and who was received through the mystery of the prophets, hidden under a veil of figures, and *was a nurse to him* [4:16], because she lacked the privileges of a mother [1222A].

made her conceive and bear a son. And the

^d souls of the saints ^e Synagogue

women^d said to Naomi^e, "Blessed be the

Lord who has not allowed your family to die

out, and his name will be known in Israel.

And you have someone to console your

spirit, and to care for you in your old age.

For he is born from your daughter-in-law

who loves you, and he is far better for you

than if you had seven sons." And Naomi

took the child and placed it on her bosom

and acted as his nurse and nanny. And,

indeed, the neighborhood women

congratulated her, saying, "A son is born to

Naomi." They named him Obed. He was the

father of Jesse the father of David. These
^f divided or separate
are the generations of Perez: Perez^f fathered
^g seeing an arrow   ^h eminent or chosen
Hezron, Hezron^g fathered Ram, Ram^h
            ^i spontaneous people
fathered Amminadab, Amminadab^i fathered
^j strong prophet
Nahshon, Nahshon^j fathered Salmon,
^k sensible   ^l strong in himself
Salmon^k fathered Boaz, Boaz^l fathered Obed,
^m serving   ^n sacrifice of a house ^o desirable one
Obed^m fathered Jesse, Jesse^n fathered David^o.

And the women . . . his name Obed] (These are) the virtuous people of the heavens who delight in the fertility of the Church; and they named him whom they desire to serve the supernal king with them Obed, that is "serving" [1222B].

He was the father of Jesse] The spiritual lineage of the race is shown here. For Obed is interpreted as "serving," Jesse as the "sacrifice of a house" or "incense," David as "strong hand" or "desirable one." For whoever serves God with strength is a pleasing sacrifice to him and is incense of sweetest odor, and devotes himself to God through works of virtue and through zeal in prayer. And so, strengthened by faith and devotion, he is desirable and pleasing to God [1222C–D].

These are the generations] There are ten generations of the sons of Judah up to David. From which you know that the intention of the whole of divine Law is directed towards Christ, who was born from the seed of David; so it proclaims His coming, and the fulfillment of the Law is manifest in Him, *For Christ is the end of the Law, so that there may be righteousness for everyone who believes* (Rom. 10:4). Before the Law [is given], therefore, Jacob says, about the incarnation of Christ, *The sceptre will not depart from Judah, nor the leader from his legs, until he comes who has been sent* (Gen. 49:10). However, to David, who is the tenth of the seed of Judah, it was said, *From the fruit of your womb, shall I place upon your throne* (Ps. 131:11). It is clear, therefore that the oracle of all prophets and patriarchs refers to the overlordship of our Lord Jesus Christ [1223A–1224A].

Notes

1. The Rabanus Maurus version is stronger: ". . . signifies that the people's possession is nothing other than the marriage of the Church with Christ."

2. The Hebrew meaning of Leah is uncertain here. Although it literally means "weak-eyed," it can also be translated as "soft-eyed" or "beautiful of eye" (Gen. 29:17).

3. Rabanus Maurus reads "figuram" not "gratiam."

4. Although Boaz called him by his name, we are not told what this was. The Hebrew tradition says that, because the man was not willing to do his duty by Ruth, he was not worthy to be named.

5. "Name": literally "seed."

6. Jerome's translation is clear here: the man undoes his own (*suum*) sandal. Other writers lost the reflexive pronoun, letting in much confusion about who was to do what to whom.

Additions to The Ordinary Gloss

CHAPTER 1

There was a famine in the land. Famine was decreed by heaven for the world ten times[1] from the Creation to the time of the Messiah, to castigate the inhabitants of the earth. The first famine was when Adam was living, when the earth was cursed for his deed (Gen. 3). The second famine happened when Lamech lived (Gen. 5). The third was when Abraham was living, when he was forced to go to Egypt (Gen. 12). The fourth was when Isaac, who went to Abimelech the king of the Palestinians, to take care of himself and his family, lived (Gen. 26). The fifth, when Jacob lived, was when he likewise sent his sons again into Egypt, on account of the grain harvest (Gen. 42). The sixth was when Boaz, a just man from Bethlehem in Judah who was kinsman to Abesan, lived (Ruth 1). The seventh was when David was king of the Israelites (2 Sam. 21). The eighth was when Elijah was the prophet (1 Kings 17). The ninth was when Elisha was living, when an ass's head came to Samaria for eighty pieces of silver, and the fourth part of a cab of doves' dung for five pieces of silver (2 Kings 6).[2] The tenth famine is still to come—not a famine of food or drink, but of hearing the word of divine prophecy.

Chaldaeus Paraphrastes [*Targum Ruth*: *SO*, p. 90; *AB*, p. 18; cf. *Midrash Rabbah. Ruth*, I.4]

He was called Elimelech. The Hebrews' tradition is that this is he in whose time the sun stood still, on account of those who did not keep the Law, so that, when they had seen such a miracle, they should turn to the Lord God. And because they scorned to do such a thing, therefore the famine grew worse, and he who seemed foremost in the tribe of Judah not only was expelled from his native land with his wife and sons, made helpless by famine, but even continued in that same exile with his sons.

Jerome, *Quaestiones Hebraicae in Paralipomenon* [*PL* 23:1373]

Elimelech. Hahalai, son of Sesan, is that same Elimelech, father of Maalon and Chilion. And Sesan is said not to have sons, because *they* died without sons.

Jerome, ibid. [*PL* 23:1368]

Elimelech. Elimelech, unable to bear the famine, migrated to the land of the Moabites, taking his wife and the sons born from her. And when everything went well there, he gave his sons Moabite wives.[3]

Josephus, *Antiquities*, bk 5, c. 9, p. 140

They took. They took foreign wives for themselves, transgressing the decree of the divine oracle;[4] and because of that they died prematurely in an ill-omened land, and left Naomi a widow, bereft of her two sons.[5]

Chaldaeus Paraphrastes (*SO*, pp. 90–91; *AB*, p. 20)

And she arose. Naomi, bearing bitterly what came to her, and unable to bear the desolation of her dear sons (for whom, it seemed, she had left her native land) returned to it.

Josephus, *Antiquities*, bk 5, c. 9, p. 140

The Lord had looked after. The Lord removed the harsh famine and gave food to Israel, on account of righteousness and of prayers which the judge Abesan, who was called pious Boaz, sent up in the sight of the Lord.

Chaldaeus Paraphrastes (*SO*, p. 91; *AB*, p. 20)

Ruth stuck by her. The constancy of Ruth, who because of the piety of her spirit and the memory of her husband preferred to her parents a woman worn out in old age, and laboring in poverty, is praiseworthy.

Theodoret, *Quaestiones in Ruth* [*PG* 80:522, no. 348]

She answered. Ruth said: Do not fight to make me desert you, because I have turned around in order to be a proselyte.[6]
Naomi said: We are ordered to keep the sabbath and the holy days, so that one may not walk more than two thousand cubits.
Ruth answered: Wherever you go, I will go.
Naomi said: We are ordered not to live with foreigners.
Ruth answered: Wherever you live, I will live.
Naomi said: We are ordered to keep the six hundred and thirteen precepts.
Ruth answered: Whatever your people observe, I will observe, exactly as if they had always been my people.
Naomi said: We are ordered not to worship a foreign God.
Ruth answered: Your God will be my God.
Naomi said: For us there are four types of death for the wicked: stoning, burning, death by the sword, and crucifixion.[7]
Ruth answered: However, you die, I will die.
Naomi said: We are buried.
Ruth answered: May I be buried in the same place. And do not speak more on this matter, for may I perish if even death separates me from you.

Chaldaeus Paraphrastes (*SO*, pp. 92–93; *AB*, p. 22)

She answered. Boaz married Ruth on account of the merits of her faith, because she scorned her own people and land and nation and chose Israel, and because she did not despise her mother-in-law, a widow like herself, and an exile; but she was led by desire to her [Naomi's] people rather than to her [Ruth's] own. She rejected the gods of her native land and chose the living God, saying to her mother-in-law, *Do not oppose me.*

Ps.-Chrysostom, *Opus Imperfectum*, hom. 1
[*PG* 56:619]

She answered. Ruth entered the Church and was made an Israelite, and deserved to be counted amongst God's greatest servants; chosen on account of the kinship of her soul, not of her body. We should emulate her because, just as she deserved this prerogative because of her behavior, we also, through our choice of behavior, may be counted among the favored elect in the Church of the Lord etc. Continuing in our Father's house, we might, through her example, say to him who, like Paul or any other bishop, calls us to worship God, *Your people are my people, and your God my God.*

Ambrose, *Comm. on Luke*, III, c. 30, *SC* 45, p. 137

CHAPTER 2

There was a kinsman. He was a kinsman of Naomi herself, of her husband, a zealous and devout man of the family of Elimelech, named Boaz.

Chaldaeus Paraphrastes (*AB*, p. 24)

To her mother-in-law. Does this widow Naomi, who sustained her widowhood by the gleanings of a foreigner who nourished her mother-in-law in her old age, seem insignificant to you? For this also works towards the aid and the grace of widows: that they teach their daughters-in-law how to help them in the fulness of their years and so, like the schoolmaster's stipend, they take the profit of their teaching. Indeed Ruth, who was well instructed and preferred her mother-in-law's widowhood to her paternal home, could not fail her. Even when her husband was dead as well, she still did not leave her, but nourished her poverty and gave solace to her mourning; nor did she who had been abandoned, herself abandon [Naomi]. The best teaching knows no want. Naomi, having lost her two sons and her husband, had not lost the profits of her piety, for she discovered a solace for mourning and an aid for poverty.

Ambrose, *Liber de viduis*, c. 6 [*PL* 16:244–45]

Hear me, daughter. This story of Boaz also teaches us about virtue. For he not only liberally shares his grain with Ruth but also consoles her with words. Not only does he share food with her but also was himself the minister of his kindness; so that whoever does not order another person to be his minister, but prepares the flour and bread himself, will have given very liberally indeed.

Theodoret, *Quaestiones in Ruth* [*PG* 80:522, no. 348]

He answered her. Boaz said to Ruth, "What is to come was signified to me by prophecy: that kings and prophets will be born from you, on account of the goodness which you have shown abundantly to your mother-in-law, whom you cared for when your husband died, even giving up your own religion, your people, your father and mother, and the land of your birth; and you endeavor to become a convert and live amongst a people who are only recently known to you. May the Lord repay you with a just reward in this world, on account of your noble deed, and your reward will be completed by the Lord God of Israel in the world to come. Moreover, your righteousness itself will free you from the judgement of Gehenna, so that you will have your portion with Sara, Rebecca, Rachael and Leah." Then Ruth said, "You are indeed merciful to me, my Lord, by speaking to fortunate me, so that I might be received in the house of the Lord; and even speaking as a man you consoled me. In these things you bear faith to me from the world to come, where reward comes to merit."[8]

Chaldaeus Paraphrastes (*SO*, pp. 94–95; *AB*, pp. 26–28)

The Lord repays you. The blessing followed as Boaz said it would. For Ruth received the full reward from God, so that she was the progenitrix of the blessing of the nations.

Theodoret, *Quaestiones in Ruth* [*PG* 80:522, no. 348]

And Naomi replied. With a heart thankful for the remembrance of kindness, Noami rewarded the absent benefactor of her daughter-in-law with a blessing. For she said, "May he who has acknowledged you be blessed, for he has filled an empty soul by doing what he did. He took notice not of

poverty but only of the Lawgiver, who ordered that widows be shown care."

Theodoret, *Quaestiones in Ruth* [*PG* 80:522, nos. 348–49)

And Naomi replied. "May he be blessed by the holy mouth of the Lord, for he kept up his kindness towards the living and the dead."

Chaldaeus Paraphrastes (*SO*, p. 96; *AB*, p. 30)

CHAPTER 3

When, however. What does Naomi suggest to her daughter-in-law? When Ruth heard her mother-in-law saying, "Our neighbor is a true man," she was reminded of his great kindness, and thought to want him [to be] married to her in law, so that she might keep up the memory of the dead. Therefore, she [Naomi] suggests to her that she sleep at Boaz's feet, not that she might sell her body (for the words of the narrative signify the opposite); rather, she trusts the man's temperance and judgement. Moreover, the actions corroborate the words.

Theodoret, *Quaestiones in Ruth* [*PG* 80:522–23, no. 349]

Wash yourself. Wash yourself and anoint yourself with pleasant oils and put on a beautiful dress and go down to the threshing floor.

Chaldaeus Paraphrastes (*SO*, p. 97; *AB*, p. 30)

Wash yourself. Abraham ben Ezra, Anoint yourself with good-smelling oil. For thus was the custom in the land of Israel: the important people, men and women, anointed themselves.[9]

When Boaz had eaten. Boaz took care of his body with food and drink, and with a sober heart[10] he blessed the name of the Lord who had listened to his prayer and had made the famine in the land of Israel cease; and he went to sleep on the outside of the heap. In the middle of the night, however, he became afraid, and his body appeared shrivelled as a radish,[11] because of fear. Moreover, seeing the woman sleeping at his feet he restrained his desire so that he did not have sex with her, in imitation of that just man Joseph.

Chaldaeus Paraphrastes (*SO*, pp. 97–98; *AB*, p. 32)

You are blessed. He praised Ruth's deed and, moreover, he did not betray temperance, but he kept to the law of nuptial congress.[12] "You show by your deed," he said, "that this was not done out of voluptuousness. In fact, you might have gone to those who are young and blooming, with only the intent of enjoying voluptuousness, but you went to the man who stands in place of a father to you." Twice indeed, he calls her daughter.

Theodoret, *Quaestiones in Ruth* [*PG* 80:523, nos 349–50]

Addition, not Theodoret:
Christ ate and drank when, in the meal of his body and blood, He gave the sacraments to the apostles. Whence, *Because the young people shared flesh and blood, He himself shared with them* [Hebr. 2:14].

Spread your blanket. "I ask that your name fall upon your handmaid, that you might take me to wife, since you are my kinsman."[13]

Chaldaeus Paraphrastes (*SO*, p. 98; *AB*, p. 32)

Unless God's inspiration had been in Ruth, she would not have said what she said, nor done what she did. What is praised in her first? A love of the tribe of Israel,[14] or obedience, or faith? She desired to have sons[15] out of the seed of Israel and become one of the people of God. Simplicity [is praised] also, because she came in under Boaz's coverlet voluntarily; she feared neither that he would perhaps spurn her, as a just man might spurn a lascivious woman, nor that he might deceive her and, worse, despise a deceived woman, as many men might have done. But, obeying her mother-in-law's plans, she confidently believed that God would prosper her action, knowing her conscience, because lust did not push her to it but rather religion was her encouragement.

What, however, is praised in Boaz? Humility, chastity, and religion. Humility indeed and chasti-

ty, because he did not touch her as a lascivious man would [touch] a girl, nor abhor her as a chaste man would a lascivious girl, but as soon as he had heard her speak of the Law, he ascribed her actions to religion. Nor did he despise her as a rich man would a pauper, nor was he in awe of her, as a mature man might be of a young woman; but, more experienced in faith than in body, he proceeded in the morning to the gate, calling the neighborhood together, and prevailing not by the law of kinship to her but, rather, by the favor of being the chosen one of God.[16]

Ps.-John Chrysostom, *Opus Imperfectum*, hom. 1 [*PG* 56:619]

Addition, not Chrysostom:
And she, in asking that his coverlet be stretched over her, was worthy to receive a blessing. For whoever receives the grace of full faith will equally possess blessing and virtue.

Stretch out. Boaz said, "Show me the linen that covers you. What measure of grain does it hold?" When it was held out, six measures of grain were placed on it. Was sufficient strength given to her by the Lord to carry it? And immediately it was believed through the prophecy that from her would spring six just men who were the future for the world, each of whom was blessed with six blessings: David, Daniel, Azariah, Hananiah, Mishael, and the King Messiah.

Chaldaeus Paraphrastes (*SO*, p. 100; *AB*, p. 34)

CHAPTER 4

Boaz went up. He went up to the gate of the assembly of the senators and sat there with the elders.

Chaldaeus Paraphrastes (*SO*, p. 100; *AB*, p. 34)

Boaz went up. The man was so virtuous that he did not rush into a marriage outside the Law, but he spoke with his neighbors about the marriage. However, his words are also worthy of admiration. For his first words were not about the marriage, but about the possession of fields etc. Moreover when, on account of the prospective marriage he [the relative] in fact refused the contract for the land, and indeed took off his sandal and gave it to Boaz, in accordance with the Law, Boaz then took Ruth to be his wife. Furthermore, because he was not serving lust, he took her in the spirit that one should take a wife, and his words also showed themselves worthy of praise, *You are witnesses today* etc. "I do not," he said, "transgress the Law in marrying a Moabite woman; rather, I diligently fulfil divine Law, so that the memory of the dead is not extinguished."

Theodoret, Quaestiones in Ruth [PG 80:523–26, nos. 350–51]

I cede my right. "I judge that I am not able to redeem her myself[17] for, since I have a wife, it is not suitable for me to add another, because discord will be stirred up in my house on account of it, and I might jeopardize the position of my heirs. Redeem her yourself since you have no wife, seeing that I am not able to redeem her."

Chaldaeus Paraphrastes (SO, p. 101; AB, p. 36)

All the people. The elders confirmed the marriage with a blessing, saying, *The Lord made this woman* etc. Moreover, *So that she may be an example of virtue in Ephrathah*, predicted the salvific birth through which Bethlehem was made famous among all people.

Theodoret, Quaestiones in Ruth [PG 80:526, no. 351]

All the people. Those things which happened to Ruth should be seen as figures. For she was an outsider and had fallen into extreme penury; but Boaz, seeing her, did not despise her on account of her poverty nor was he horrified on account of her impiety; even as Christ received the Church, who was both a stranger and laboring, in need of great good things. Ruth is not joined with her consort before forsaking her parents and her nation and her native land: never was anyone so much ennobled by marriage. Thus the Church was not made love-able to her spouse before she had forsaken her prior customs. The prophet says, *Forget your people* (Ps. 45:10).

John Chrysostom, Homeliae in Matthaeum, no. 3, pp. 36–37 [PG 57:35–36]

All the people. Boaz took Ruth to be his wife because of the merits of her faith, so that a royal nation might be born out of so holy a marriage. For Boaz, an old man, did not take a wife for himself but for God; not on account of his corporeal passions, but on account of the justice of the law, to revive the seed of his kinsman. not serving love so much as religion. He was old in age but youthful in faith.

Ps.-John Chrysostom, Opus Imperfectum, hom. 1 [PG 56:619]

The women whom Scripture censures are placed in the genealogy of the Savior so that someone who is worshipped on account of sinners [and is] born from sinners washes out the sins of all people. From which Ruth the Moabitess was placed there, and also Bathsheba the wife of Uriah.

Jerome, Commentaire sur S. Matthieu, c. 1 (S.C., no. 242, p. 72)

Ruth, a foreigner, did not leave Naomi's side. See how much merit there is in standing by the deserted in solace. From her seed, Christ is born.

Jerome, Letters, no. 39, to Paula: Epitaph Blesilae (CSEL 54, pp. 304–05)

I have, then, explained these things which Ruth did, wishing to show the power of God who can raise anything He wishes to the summit of dignity, and there He led even David, who was born of low origins.

Josephus, Antiquities, bk 5, c. 9, p. 141

Translated from the Lyons, 1589 edition of
Biblia sacra, cum glossa ordinaria.

Notes

1. Ten is a commonly significant Old Testament number: for example, the ten plagues of Egypt or the ten commandments. The Targums to Ruth, Esther, and the Song of Songs all begin with different lists of tens.

2. I.e., famine had made prices extortionate. A cab was a measure.

3. This passage is rather a paraphrase of Josephus's text.

4. I.e., breaking the prohibition of Deut. 23:3, "No Ammonite or Moabite shall be admitted to the assembly of the Lord."

5. Note here and elsewhere the Jewish commentators' need to justify the bad things that happen to apparently good people. It is important for them to show that an evil outcome is not merely caprice on God's part but a just reward.

6. The text plays on her physical turning round to follow Naomi, and her spiritual turning around to follow Naomi's religion. Note here as elsewhere a Jewish form of exegesis by constructing extra scenes or dialogue for the biblical characters, in an attempt to explain a contracted or compressed story.

7. This is the Targum list. See Nicholas of Lyra's commentary for a slightly different list of four types of death.

8. The Targum is itself unclear here. *AB* reads, "For you have comforted me, by pronouncing me worthy, to be acceptable in the congregation of the Lord. And for speaking comforts in the heart of your maidservant in assuring me the refuge of the world to come as in righteousness" (p. 28).

9. This sole reference to Abraham ben Ezra (Ibn Ezra, ca. 1089–1164), Jewish grammarian, theologian, poet and philosopher, is tantalizing. Ibn Ezra wrote commentaries, largely from a grammatical perspective, on the Hebrew Bible text, but it is not clear that they were translated into Latin, or indeed, if this comment is not simply a fairly standard note that could have been culled from elsewhere (Andrew of St. Victor, for instance, has some striking parallels to Ibn Ezra), or heard from a Jewish scholar orally.

10. *Targum Ruth* reads, "with a merry heart." By translating the word as "sober," the Gloss must be making a deliberate point, and leaving the reader in no doubt that Boaz did not act out of drunkenness.

11. Apparently this is a strange figure of speech even in the Aramaic, which likens his body to rapeseed (*SO*, p. 98, n. 1).

The reader is reminded that there would be no possible double meaning to "rape" in the original language.

12. I.e., no sex before marriage.

13. Another roundabout saying in the Aramaic. The *Targum Ruth* is explaining the phrase "spread your blanket over me" (which meant "take me as your wife") by using another phrase "let your name fall upon me," which had the same meaning.

14. *PG* text adds "or simplicity."

15. *PG* text reads "A love of the tribe of Israel because she desired to have sons. . . ."

16. I.e., they were married not because it was the Law, and Boaz was the closer relative, but actually inspite of the Law, because God willed it.

17. The Targum refers to the closer relative as "the Redeemer," since he redeems the name of the dead man. This made a useful link for Christian exegetes, who could use it in their Christological interpretation of the text, since Christ was the Redeemer of the world.

Peter Comestor: The Scholastic History

CHAPTER 23: ON THE BOOK OF RUTH

After Samson, the priest Eli, who was known not so much as a judge than as a priest from the worthier office, judged Israel.[1] This first among the sons of Ithamar took the priesthood after the priestly office was transferred away from the sons of Eleazar. In his time, there was a famine in the land; and Elimelech, an Ephrathite, arose and went from Bethlehem with his wife Naomi and their two sons Maalon and Chilion. And he went into the country of the Moabites, there to be fed. When he died, his sons took Moabite wives, Ruth and Orpha. Josephus,[2] however, says that the father got wives for his sons; and they stayed there ten years, and they both died without children.

So Naomi, a widow, deprived of her children, arose to go back to her native land, for she had heard that the Lord had given food to His people; and her daughters-in-laws made to accompany her. She said to them, *My daughters, go back to your mothers' houses, for you cannot hope for more men from my womb.* And note that, since the law concerning the reviving of the name was observed among the Moabites, Orpha obeyed her and turned back, but Ruth still followed her.[3]

Naomi said to her, "Hear me, daughter. Our God is not like the gods of the Gentiles, nor do our people live according to Gentile rites; it is better that you return to your people and your gods." But Ruth said, *Your people are my people, and your God is my God.*

And they hastened on together and came to Bethlehem, which was first called Ephrathah, from the [name of the] wife of Caleb. According to some, she was Miriam, Moses' sister, who was taken there from the desert and who, after she was struck down with leprosy, was called Ephrath, that is, "she sees fury" (that is, she has known God's anger from that deed); or else it means "mirror," because her plague was set up as an example to all. However, on account of the return of its incredible fertility, it began to be called Bethlehem, which means "house of bread."

Knowledge of them spread in Bethlehem, and people said, *This is Naomi herself.* She answered them, *Call me not Naomi, which means beautiful, but call me Mara, which means bitterness. For I went out full and the Lord returned me empty, full of bitterness.*

That was the time of the first barley harvest. And there was a powerful and wealthy man there, Boaz, a kinsman of Elimelech. And with Naomi's consent, Ruth went to his fields and collected ears of grain behind the harvesters.

Now it happened that Boaz came to the field and said to the harvesters, *The Lord be with you.* And he asked them who the girl was. And they said, *She is a Moabitess who came with Naomi.* And Boaz said to her, *Daughter, do not go into anyone else's field. None of the boys will bother you. If you are thirsty, go to my young men's baggage and drink; and when the dinner hour comes, eat as well, and dip your morsel into the vinegar. The God of Israel gives you your reward, since you have taken refuge under his wings.* And he said to his boys, *Throw out some grain from your bundles so she may gather the grain without shame.*

And when Ruth had eaten with the harvesters, she gathered together the polenta (which Josephus calls "alphita"[4]), and kept it for her mother-in-law. And so in the evening, beating out what she had gathered with a rod, she had an ephah's worth of barley, that is, three measures. And when she returned to her mother-in-law she told her what Boaz had done. And Naomi said, *Our neighbor is a true man; let him be blessed by God.*

Ruth did the same thing on the following days, right up to the time for winnowing. The custom in Israel was for the lord to prepare a grand feast at the winnowing floor for his boys and harvesters. And he slept on the floor and abstained from women, quasi-religiously.[5] The same thing was done at sheep-shearing time. If it was the same after the grape-harvest, I have not read it.

And Naomi said to Ruth, *Wash yourself, daughter, and anoint yourself and put on your Sunday best, and go to the threshing floor with the others. The man may not see you until he has eaten and drunk. And when he is sleeping, tuck yourself in by his feet and lie there.* And she did all these things which her mother-in-law ordered. And behold, in the middle of the night the man woke up, and was afraid, saying, *Who are you?* And she answered, *I am your handmaiden. Spread your cloak over me, because you are my kinsman.* And when Boaz had declared to her that chastity would be safeguarded in such an unlawful situation, he added, *There is another who is a closer kinsman to you than I am. If he wishes to hold to the law of closer kinship, all well and good; otherwise, as the Lord lives, I will receive you [into my household].*

Thus Boaz arose from the place where he lay next to the grain store before men could recognize one another, and he filled her cloak with barley—about six measures. And Ruth, returning burdened to her mother-in-law, told her what Boaz had said.

So Boaz went to the gate and sat with the judges, and called ten of the elders, and he called the closer kinsman (of whom he had spoken) to him, and he said to him, *Naomi wishes to sell part of the field of our father Elimelech. We are her only two relatives; but you are the nearer. Therefore, buy it, if you wish.* And he said, *I shall buy it.* Then Boaz said to him, "You ought not to remember only the simple part of the law;[6] for along with the field you must take Maalon's widow, to revive your kinsman's name." And he said, *I cede my right under the law of propinquity. You can have my rights.* And Boaz said, "Take [off] your sandal,

then, to seal the bargain." Josephus,[7] however, says, "Thus Boaz, with the elders as witnesses, orders the woman to remove his sandal, according to the law, and spit in his face." But John [the Baptist] says, "One whose sandals I am not worthy to untie" (John 1:27).

From these three people it may be conjectured in the various cases that whenever a man is refusing a woman he loosens his own sandal; but sometimes a woman loosens his sandal when a man is taking her under his protection. But whichever way it is done, his house is called (as the disgrace of a refugee from the Law) "the house of the unshod" (Deut. 25:10).[8] And Boaz said to those standing by, *You are witnesses to this.* They said, *We are witnesses. May the Lord make this woman to you like Rachael and Leah, who built the house of Israel.* Thus Boaz took Ruth to be his wife. And after a year a son was born to her, and Naomi held him to her bosom, and fed him and nursed him. And the neighbors congratulated her, *Behold, you have someone to nurse in your old age; and may he serve you more than seven sons.* On account of this he was called Obed, which means in Hebrew "serving." He is the father of Jesse the father of David.

Translated from *PL* 198:1293–96,
checked against Oxford, Bodleian Library,
MS Bodl. 711, fol. 72ra–vb.

Notes

1. I.e., he was both a priest and a judge, but was known as a priest because it was the worthier, that is, more dignified, office. This opening is taken from Josephus.

2. Josephus, *Antiquities*, bk 5, c. 9: see the additions to the Gloss.

3. Peter means we can tell that the custom of levirate marriage (Deut. 25:5–10) was also observed in Moab, since Orpha was going back to her own people in order to marry again and bear a son who would carry on Chilion's name.

4. Josephus, *Antiquities*, bk 5 c. 9: "alpheta."

5. This phrase, *quasi-solemnizans*, is missing from MS Oxford, BL, Bodl. 711.

6. Josephus, *Antiquities*, bk 5, c. 9.

7. Josephus, *Antiquities*, bk 5, c. 9.

8. This paragraph seems to reflect the medieval uncertainty about the sandal-loosening custom; or perhaps Peter is merely trying to simplify for the unsophisticated.

Hugh of St. Cher: Postills on Ruth

The bee is little amongst flying things (Ecclus. 11:3) and yet, a great fruit springs forth for the whole Church—wax, the food of fire; and a medicine for wounds, which is honey. In the same way, the book of Ruth is a small door in terms of the letter, but inside it is filled by the greatness of its spirit. For just as in a nut the small sweet kernel is contained within the outer shell, and as sweet honey is held in the honeycomb, or medicinal grain is stored in the granary, so in this little story of Christ and the Church, the sacraments lie hidden. For this book was written, as others are, inside and outside. The outside holds the killing letter, but the inside has the lifegiving spirit (2 Cor. 3:6). It has an historical foundation, allegorical columns built on that foundation, and a tropological architrave on top of the columns.

This story is connected to higher things because it is thought to have happened at the time of a certain judge, namely Boaz (who is also called Abesan). According to the Hebrews,[1] Ruth was the daughter of Eglon, king of Moab, whom Ehud killed (according to Judges 3). Boaz married her, as the story repeatedly says. But for that reason, it would seem that the story ought to be placed in the middle of the book of Judges, and not put in later. For it is agreed that Abesan was the ninth judge, since he is placed immediately after Jephthah (Judges 12). Therefore the Master of the Histories says that the judge after Sampson was Eli, who was not however called a judge, but a priest, on account of the greater dignity.[2] In his time there was a famine in the land, and because of this Elimelech, his wife Naomi, and his two sons Maalon and Chilion went into the country of Moab, in order to be fed. There one of the sons took Ruth, whose story is told in this book, as his wife.

And so it is clear that this book is correctly placed after Judges and before Kings, because in this book it is shown how, with Ruth, Boaz fathered Obed, who was the father of Jesse, who was the father of David the King, about whom the book of Kings is for the most part concerned. Therefore, this book is rightly placed in the middle between Kings and Judges because it is the common boundary at which the different stories are joined, as if at a point. However, according to the Hebrews, this book is not a single book in itself, but is a part of the book of Judges.[3] In fact, the reason why this book is placed with the book of Judges rather than with the book of Kings is clear, because the story happens not "at the time of a certain king" but "at the time of a certain judge," as it says in the literal sense.

But again, someone may ask why, since the book means to tell the story of Ruth and Boaz equally, it not called after Boaz rather than Ruth? Answer:[4] This was done to show the grace of Christ more strongly and clearly. For, as Jerome says, Ruth is one of the four sinful women whose names appear in the genealogy of Christ (Matt. 1).[5] Only four women sinners are named there: Tamar, Rahab, Ruth, Bathsheba. Therefore, the author means principally to show how Obed (from whom came Jesse the father of David, from whom comes Christ) was born from Ruth; and so from Ruth comes Christ. Whence (Isai. 16:1), Send lambs . . . by way of the desert, that is Ruth, a Gentile deserted by God, to the mountain of daughter Sion, that is, to the Church.

From which [it is clear that] the Father is the material cause of this book as much of the literal sense as of the spiritual. Indeed the Father is the intention of the author which turns always around the material cause.[6] However, who the author was is not explained, so we shall leave it that he is the same as the author of Judges and Kings, namely Hezechiah, who united the Chronicles of Solomon into one. The utility of the book is clear; the title of the book is clear. The method of proceeding is this: first, it is shown how Elimelech journeyed to the country of Moab, with Naomi his wife and two sons; how, after his death, the sons took wives there; how, when those sons died without heirs, Naomi returned to her own land with one daughter-in-law, namely Ruth. Second, it is shown how Boaz took Ruth as his wife, when her other, closer relative had given up his right to her. Finally, the generations of the fathers from Phares the son of Judah right up to David are recounted, at which point the next book begins, in which the succession of the books is made clear. (Rabanus expounds this book.[7])

End of the Prologue.

The Literal Sense

CHAPTER 1

In the days of a certain judge, namely Boaz, who was also called Abesan: this is how the Hebrews interpret it.[8] The Master of the Histories says that there was a famine at the time of Eli. This is really a moral interpretation, for Eli was a priest and a judge, and at that time a spiritual famine particularly began to bite, since earthly power had fallen to priests.[9] In this way Eli had usurped the priesthood using his earthly power. For first he transferred that priesthood from the sons of Eleazar (to whom it was due according to the law of primogeniture) to himself, who was of the family of Ithamar. And after that there was truly a spiritual famine in the Church, since someone had

usurped ecclesiastical dignities for himself using earthly power.

When judges ruled. This is said in this way because those who were in control and who should be pastors were made judges; and when they ought to have been free for prayer, they were free for quarrels and lawsuits. Therefore there was a famine in the Church: Amos 8:1, *I will send a famine on the land* etc. Also on this sort of thing, 1 Cor. 6 (verses 1–6 paraphrased), if you hold secular judges in contempt, who are those constituted in the Church to judge? Here is what Jethro said to Moses about the effort of judgement: You will not do good; you will be consumed by foolish labor (Exod. 18:18).

From Bethlehem, that is, [he was] a Bethlehem-dweller. And this is foreknowledge, for it was not yet called Bethlehem. Bethlehem and Ephrathah were the same town; but formerly it was called Ephrathah, after Ephrath the wife of Caleb, who was buried there. But it was later called Bethlehem, that is, house of bread, on account of the amazing fertility of the land. According to some, this Ephrath was the sister of Miriam, the wife of Moses, who was afterwards struck with leprosy (Num. 12). She was called Ephrath, which means, "she sees frenzy," that is to say, "she has known the anger of God by experience." Again, it is interpreted to mean "mirror," because her disease was given to her as an example to all. Jerome, however, says that Caleb received Hur the father of Uri, the uncle of Bezalel from Ephrathah (as is said in 1 Chron. 2 and 4).[10] Others say that it was the town that was first called "she sees frenzy" (*Ephrath*) because, at the aforesaid time of the Judges, it felt the anger of God, that is to say, a serious famine, and afterwards it was called Bethlehem, because of being so fertile.

Elimelech. On 1 Chron. 4, Jerome says that in Elimelech's time the sun stood still, to frighten transgressors of the law.[11] Because they did not fear God, such a great famine grew up that he preferred to flee from the tribe of Judah, with his wife and sons.

Orpha. She was Chilion's wife.

And the woman was left, namely Naomi.

And her husband, completely bereft.

To your mothers. She says "mother" not "father" perhaps because their fathers were dead, or because daughters are inclined to love their mothers more.

My dead family. "My family," namely, her sons and her husband.

In my womb, which is to say "I am an old woman and menstruation[12] has already ceased in me; nor am I able to conceive sons for you to have in order to revive the name[13] of their dead brothers." From this it is clear that the law about the restoration of the name, about which Deut. 25 speaks, was still kept amongst the Moabite people.

Puberty. Puberty and consent were both necessary in a contract of marriage. Puberty was marked in a man about the age of fourteen, in a woman about the age of twelve.[14]

Before you were married, that is, before you are able to marry them.

I pray you not to come all the way.

Is turned against me, namely, from his own place, that is, from pity to the justice with which he has punished me by the death of my husband and sons, just as in Isai 26:21, *For the Lord comes out from his place to punish the inhabitants of the earth for their iniquity.*

Her mother-in-law, namely Naomi, her husband's mother.

Back to her people. From this it is clear that Orpha and Ruth were not sisters.

Go with her. It would seem that Naomi sinned because she advised Ruth to remain in idolatry. Perhaps she said this thing to tempt her, to see if she was determined because, as 2 Peter 2:21 says, *It would have been better for them never to have known the way of righteousness than, after knowing it, to turn back from the holy commandment*; or it was permission, not advice or a command, because she could not compel her; or, in the mystical sense, the Synagogue is understood

by "Naomi" here, who holds back from faith whoever she can, as Rabanus says.[15]

May the Lord do these things for me. This is a prayer.

Made up her mind, that is, confirmed in her good purpose.

And they went on, that is, they began to proceed.

And came to Bethlehem. This is foreknowledge [of the name].

Knowledge of them spread, because Naomi had come.

This is Naomi herself can be read *interrogative*, as a question, or *remissive*, as a statement.[16]

Full, that is, having a husband and sons. On the other hand, we read about Jacob (Gen. 32:10), *I have crossed the Jordan with my rod and now I return with two bands.*

CHAPTER 2

Go, my daughter, this means Naomi sent her to the grain, that is, to grace, but Pharaoh (Exod. 5) sent them to the chaff, that is, to the devil.

From Bethlehem into the field.

The Lord be with you. As it says here, the priestly greeting which is said at Mass and at the Offices, is given by him. It follows the pattern of Jud. 6:12, where the angel said to Gideon, *The Lord be with you, strongest of men*; and the episcopal greeting, like that of Jud. 6:23, where the angel said to Gideon, *Peace be with you*; or from John 20:19, where the Lord says to the disciples, *Peace be with you*. And they answer the Apostle, *and with your spirit*, when he says, *Grace be with your spirit* (Philem. vv. 3, 25).

To my baggage: to the place where there were stores of bread and jugs of water and vinegar in other jars for carrying away food.

On her face. Good men fall on their faces. Their humility and discretion can be observed in this, because they can see where they fall, for example, Apoc. 7, *And all the angels fell on their faces before the throne and worshipped God*; and Ezech. 1:28, *And I fell on my face*. Bad men, however, fall backwards, as in 1 Sam. 4:18, Eli fell from his chair backwards; and in John 18:6, it is said about those who came to take the Lord, *They stepped back and fell to the ground*.

Why have I found favor? Behold, she humbled herself like the centurion (Matt. 8:8), *Lord I am not worthy*, etc., as Elizabeth says in Luke 1. And thence, *Upon me alone, my Lord, be the guilt*, as Abigail says in 1 Sam. 25:24.

Of your husband or "her husband."[17]

Wings, "protection."

Barley-flour, that is, a bundle of grain, which in French is called *grenee*. Josephus calls it *afficam*.[18]

And from then on, that is, "from that place where they ate"; or else "then" is to mean "after that."

Cutting and shaking out: "and" used to mean "that is."[19]

Of an ephah, which is the tenth part of a cor. A cor, however, holds thirty measures, as Ezech. 45:11–14 says.

And again she said. And she tells Ruth to finish, for she did not wish to tear her young mind away from religion.

CHAPTER 3

Until he has finished. The custom in Israel was that the lord held a great feast on the threshing floor for his boys and for his winnowers, and he slept on the threshing floor, abstaining from the embraces of women that night. The same thing happened at sheep-shearing and after the grape harvest, according to some sources, but we do not read of that here.[20]

Next to the pile of hay. A pile of sheaves of grain built into a point at the top.[21]

Latest pity. The first instance of pity was that she followed Naomi; the second instance was that she wished to revive the name of her dead husband. The argument is that pity is greater when done for the dead than for the living, because the living can help themselves in some way, but the dead cannot.

I do not deny, that is, I concede or recognize.

As the Lord lives. This is the form of an oath.

Before men knew each other, lest she be judged at all unfavorably.

Stretch out. He did this so she might seem to have come from the field where she had been reaping.

CHAPTER 4

Boaz went up to the town gate where judgements were made and matters were aired. For the judges were ordered to sit there (Deut. 16:18) so that they might be available to everyone; and they gave justice openly, unlike those today who keep themselves hidden.

Our father Elimelech. Elimelech was called "father" because he was the eldest.[22]

Buy it and have it. But how could he buy it? Did it not say in the same sentence that Naomi had sold the field? *Answer*: Naomi sold the field when she left, under a kind of contract whereby she might get it back again on her return, or under the type of contract where it could be bought back by her closest kinsman, as the law allows in France.[23] Or [we can explain it] by expounding "has sold," as meaning "has for sale."

To keep alive the name. According to the Law in Deut 25:5.

I cede my right. It is argued that, according to the Law, whoever was the closer relative by blood was the first to inherit. He wanted the inheritance, however, but not to revive the name [of his dead kinsman].

For I should not harm. Here it tells us that the first male child was said to be the son of the dead man.

The man undid his own sandal. Josephus[24] says that Boaz told the woman to loosen his sandal and spit in his [the kinsman's] face, according to the Law which said that whenever anyone wished to divorce he loosened his own sandal; whenever a woman was being divorced, she loosened his sandal; when the man who was marrying her . . . and so on in various cases. . . .[25] For example, when a man gave up his right of his own free will, and there was no objection, then he took off his own sandal. But when the woman objected, in front of the judges, she took off the sandal and spat in his face, as Deut. 25 says. But when a man who ought to have married a woman rejected her, and she objected that he ought to take her by the Law of the nearest kinsman, then, in this case, he himself took off his sandal to reject her. According to which John the Baptist said (John 1:27), *I am not worthy to untie the thong of his sandal*. But according to this it seems that Boaz ought to have taken off the relative's sandal because Boaz made the objection. *Answer*: Boaz did not object over the contract of marriage, but he said that if he wished to buy the field he must take Ruth as his wife as well, not explaining that he himself wanted to marry her; because if he had said that, then he ought to have taken off the relative's sandal. However, it could be the case that it was a disgrace to have one's sandal removed, and one's house was called the house of the barefoot (Deut. 25:10).[26]

Like Rachel, loved and fertile.

The house of Israel that is, Jacob.

So that she, namely, Ruth herself.

In Ephrathah, that is, Bethlehem.

Whom Tamar bore: Gen. 38.

And the women said, after Ruth had given birth.

Your family. He wanted it complete so that *his name might be known* etc.

To care for you in your old age, that is, to keep you in your old age; for which reason he was called Obed, which means "serving." About which Chrysostom on Matt. 1 says, "Obed is interpreted to mean '"subject'."[27] Nowadays, however, people choose riches and not morals, good looks and not

faithfulness, and what it is usual to ask of harlots they look for in wives; moreover, they father sons who are servants neither of themselves nor of God, but who are arrogant, so that they are not the fitting fruit of a marriage but the penalty of irreligion.

Than seven sons, not subjects, because they believed the son to be subject to Him to whom they saw his mother was subject.

The Allegorical/Mystical Sense

Chapter 1

There was a famine. There was a famine of the word of God on account of the scarcity of those learned in spiritual things, to whom the authority to judge is given; and the Law was corrupted by Judaic traditions.

And a man went out. According to certain commentators,[28] the man represents the ten commandments, his wife is the Synagogue, and his two sons were kingly and priestly power, who got wives for themselves not only from amongst the Jewish people but even from amongst the proselytes, just as happened in David's and Solomon's times, and that of some others. Or the man is Christ.

To exile, because Christ was born in Bethlehem (Ps. 87:5, *This one and that one were born in it*) in Judea, when he visited the pilgrimage[29] of this world (Ps. 119:19) with the apostles and the prophets: *Your statutes have been my songs wherever I make my home* (Ps. 119:54). Or [it means] Judea, where he died, fulfilling the Law, and was made obedient unto death (Phil. 2:8).

Elimelech is interpreted as "my god and king." This is Christ, of whom it is said, *Listen to the sound of my cry, my king and my God* (Ps. 5:2).

His wife Naomi is the Church.

Two sons, prophets and apostles.

Maalon is interpreted as meaning "from the window" or "from the beginning." This is the chorus of prophets through whom the first light of faith comes into the world, as though through a window. They were indeed the first heralds of the true light, that is, of Christ.

Chilion is interpreted as meaning "fulfillment." This is the chorus of apostles who lead the dark sayings of the prophets into the consummation of complete understanding. Whence John 4:38, *Others have labored, and you have entered in to their labor.*

Ephrathites, that is, "bearing fruit," because both bore much fruit. For this purpose they were sent (John 15:16, *I appointed you to go and bear fruit, fruit that will last*), and they were called children[30] because they were freed by the blood of Christ from the slavery of sin.

From Bethlehem, because you chose the bread that satisfies: through the preaching of the Gospel, they led many to the confession of faith, so that they were fulfilled. Whence, *You give them something to eat* (Luke 9:13).

Wives, of the two sons of Elimelech: the two peoples whom Christ brought to fulfillment after his death through the prophets and apostles, since he sent the apostles to preach.

Orpha: "her neck." These are the faithful Jews who were the first to perceive the strength of faith and the power of good deeds.

Ruth: "seeing" or "hurrying" or "ceasing"; in whom the obedience and faith of the Gentiles is depicted: Ps. 18:43, *People whom I had not known served me*, and Ps. 68:31, *Let Ethiopia hasten to stretch out its hands to God.* From them was made one sheepfold (John 10:16).

Ten years: the apostles and the prophets fulfilling the ten commandments.

Both died, in this exile; so that they received the ten beatitudes to fulfil the ten commandments.

And the woman was left, after the Lord's ascension and the apostles's suffering.

The woman, that is, the Church.

Deprived, in this present, bodily sense.

Native land: the heavens.

With both her daughters-in-law, that is, with both peoples. But the Synagogue remained in unbelief, while the Gentile Church stuck firmly to Christ. From her was born Obed, who is interpreted as meaning "serving God," that is, as his faithful people.

Go home. The Church does not act indiscriminately nor receive anyone into herself indiscriminately: 1 John 4:1, *Do not believe every spirit, but test the spirits to see whether they are from God.* Alternatively, they may join with the Synagogue which held back from coming to the faith of Christ; or, *Go home to your mothers*, that is, to concupiscence. In this case, their father is the devil (Ezech. 16:45, *Your father was an Amorite*). How much better does he receive those who forsake their father and their mother and join with him! In what way, therefore, does the Church encourage people to desire those things from which it ought rather to call them back? It must be remembered that one "speaks" not only by words but also by deeds, e.g., Titus 1:16, *They confess that they know God, but by deeds they deny him.* After Christ died, both the apostles and the other saints denied him; not everyone may teach the Church in this way, and revive the name of our dead brother, that is, Christ, by these means. In these things, that is sadness, bitterness, bereavement, barrenness, and even perversity in some people, the works of the Church seem as if they would rather persuade people that they ought to return to concupiscence. For just as beauty, prosperity, fertility and rich teaching once converted many, in the same way now the deformity, adversity, and sterility of the Church perverts many and makes them turn away. Whence, Job 19, comparing the time of Christ and the apostles when the Church was blessed, and the present state as she cries out in pain: *Oh, that I were as in the months of old, as in the days when God watched over me; when his lamp shone over my head, and I was walking by that light through darkness* (Job 29:2–3). Again, Lament. 4:1, *How the gold has grown dim!*

We will go with you. Orpha and Ruth signify local churches who seek from Naomi, as if from a mother, husbands for the Church, that is, good prelates. To which Naomi replies:

Go back . . . Do I have more sons in my womb? Which is to say "I do not have in the chapter[31] anyone worthy, of and suitable for, the guidance of souls."

Already an old woman. And in this way the Church is overwhelmed, for few men marry the Church as men do, but more do it like lions.[32] For they do not look for children by her, but for carnal delight, they do not look for fruit but for a gift; although the apostle says the opposite in Phil. 4:17, *Not that I seek the gift.* This is said on account of the boys who are put in charge of churches. Before they are grown up, the churches are old and worn out, and they always remain barren unless they fornicate with heretics or certainly with demons. And this was signifed in Gen. 38:11 where Judah says to Tamar, his daughter-in-law, *Stay a widow until my son Selah grows up.* But Tamar, unwilling to wait so long, put on the clothes of a harlot, and made herself a whore. Just so, today, churches commit much spiritual fornication because bishops say to them, *Stay a widow until Selah my nephew grows up,*[33] and meanwhile they themselves take the fruit of the churches. Such bishops are complained of in Job 21:7–8, *Why do the wicked live on, reach old age, and grow mighty in power.* Their name is established in their sight, that is, they conceive a crowd of relatives and nephews in darkness. This is well-said, because such men do not dare to put boys in charge openly, but only secretly, because whoever does evil hates the light (John 3:20). This is what we read in Gen. 19:30–38, that Lot fathered Moab and Ammon by night. Lot is interpreted to mean "turning away"; he is a prelate turning away from good. He fathered Moab and Ammon, meaning that brothers and relatives are put in charge. Ammon is interpreted as "son of my people": behold my children; but Moab means "from the father":

behold the brothers. Today, bishops put such men in charge and few others. But so what? Surely those appointed are innocent, for the sin is in the doer? For example, when Jotham (that is, "gift of the dove," namely of the holy Spirit), reproved the Shechemites (Jud. 9:18) because they put his brother Abimelech in charge because of his parentage, he said, *You made Abimelech, son of a maidservant, king over the inhabitants of Shechem because he is your brother.* Mich. 3:1, *Listen, you heads of Jacob, and rulers of the house of Israel. Is it not for you to know judgement?* Again, David means "good prelate": Ps. 16:4, *I will not gather in their meeting-places.* He says "meeting-places" because certain bishops have nephews in their houses in flocks. Job 21:11, *They send out their little ones like a flock.* From this, Isai. 66:8 wondered, *Who has heard of such a thing?*

Or again: Do I have more sons in my womb? Allegorically, this is the voice of the Synagogue confessing the truth and not being silent about her overwheening fault: that she had been abandoned by a man (that is, David), left bereft and bereaved of her sons, that is, of the kings and princes. She is feeble and barren in bearing spiritual sons after the coming of Christ.

Sons: believers in Christ.

Turn back to keeping the laws.

Orpha . . . turned back to the ceremonies or the error of idolatry.

Ruth stuck by her mother-in-law. These two women signify believers, some of whom return to sin after baptism, but others persevere in grace.

Wherever you go. In this way the Church of the Gentiles declares that she will go wherever the flesh of Christ ascends; and she declares that she wishes to suffer in his name with the holy people. Whence Isaiah (cf. Isai. 66:10) or, according to another letter, *Praise, O nations, his people* (Deut. 32:43).

Your people: through merits,

Are my people, by the aid of grace alone, by a free choice.

Land: of those living corporally.

And came to Bethlehem. Naomi, that is, the primitive Church,[34] led Ruth, that is, the church of the Gentiles [to Bethlehem], that is, to the faith of Christ, and she united her to Boaz, whose name means "strong," that is, to Christ who plundered strongly the belongings of the "strong man" and distributed the spoils (Matt. 12:29; Mark 3:27; Luke 11:22).

Call me not. He does not love present joys placed in the press of this world but he seeks future glory (Song 1:5, *I am black but comely. . . . Do not gaze on me for I am dark*). Or [it means] the Synagogue confesses the truth herself.

When the first barley was being harvested. The barley harvest is explained as the time of our Lord's passion, which is the month of new things, that is next to the first month.[35] The Gentiles, therefore, come to faith at the time that the Law predicts that Christ (whom it teaches was born in Bethlehem), would die; it preaches that He died at Passover, that is in the month of new things; His incarnation and resurrection is a mystery the Church works hard to imbue her own people with.

Or the barley harvest is the faithful people from amongst the Jews who, when the sacrament of the passion had been completed, were the first to come to faith by the preaching of the apostles; they were chosen to be fed five barley loaves by the Lord (John 6).

Or the barley harvest is the conversion of sinners (of whatever sort) in the recollection of the suffering of Christ. Again, barley is the food of the sick. Whence the Lord first of all satisfied five thousand men with five barley loaves (John 6:13); secondly, four thousand men with seven loaves of wheat (Mark 8:5); thirdly, He fed the disciples with the feast of His own body (Luke 22). Through this may be noted the triple order of the elect, whom the Lord fed: with barley, [He fed] the penitent (who, although they were refreshed by the hope of pardon, were however pricked by the bitterness of penitence); by wheat is signified the just

or those professing the faith (who already delight in penitence without pricking); through the feast of his body, the perfect or contemplative are signified (who are indeed to some extent filled up with the vision of God on this earth).

CHAPTER 2

There was a kinsman. Christ was born into human flesh from the Jewish people (Deut. 18:15, *The Lord your God will raise up for you a prophet*).

Power, because He subdued the princes of the earth and brought the whole world under His control (Ps. 24:8, *The Lord, strong and mighty*).

Of great wealth, because the Lord is the possessor of the heavens and the earth. In Him all the treasures of wisdom and knowledge have been concealed (Col. 2:3). *He is the father of virtue and wisdom* (1 Cor. 1:30).

Boaz: The fortitude of God (Isai. 9:6, *And he is named Wonderful Counsellor, Mighty God*; Ps. 118:14, *The Lord is my strength and my might*).

Into a field: the Church, where the seeds of the virtues grow and the corn of glory is harvested. The harvesters are preachers, the ears of corn are souls. The harvesters gather bundles of cornstalks, because the great doctors make great fruit; but to Ruth, that is, to the friars preachers, it suffices to collect single ears of grain, that is, to convert any souls to God by preaching far and wide to the world at large. And often it happens that he who preaches this way converts many more than he who preaches with subtlety. Whence Shamgar killed six hundred by his ploughshare, but Ehud killed only Eglon by his polished sword (Jud. 3:31).

Or the field is Scripture and the harvest is subtle teachings; the harvesters who separate the grain from the chaff are the doctors who, having a rich vein to work on, grasp many things in a short time. Ruth signifies the Minors who gather the gleanings (that is the rough teaching which the great doctors leave behind), from which they make polenta, with which they feed Naomi, that is, the Church. And the ears of grain are likened to the opinions of sacred Scripture because there are three parts to an ear of grain: the pricking whiskers, the worthless chaff, and the grain for eating. And so there are three parts to any teaching: painful study, the literal sense (which may appear worthless), and the nourishing mystery. The Lord of this field was Boaz, that is, Christ.

Or else [it can mean] the field is the world and the harvest is the end of time, or the death of any just person resting in the celestial granary; and the harvesters are angels (Matt. 13:39).

Gleanings. The remaining ears of grain are those faithful people who, when the rest have been translated to heaven, remain with us as an example.

Wherever you meet with kindness. Thus should the harvesters (that is, the doctors of theology) show kindness, and forbid no one from collecting corn (that is, from expounding any opinion). Deut. 24:19, *When you forget a sheaf in the field, you should not go back to get it*, that is, when you are expounding opinions and you leave something unexpounded, do not go back to deal with it then, but allow a stranger or pupil or widow to deal with it; that is, do not prohibit exposition in ways other than you expound. The same is said about olives and vines: sacred Scripture is called wheat because it feeds and comforts; it is called wine because it gladdens and inebriates; it is called oil because it heals, gives light and makes fat. About the first, the Psalm says (Ps. 104:15) *Bread to strengthen the human heart*. In the same place (Ps. 104:15) about the second thing, *And wine to gladden the human heart*, and also *My cup overflows* (Ps. 23:5). About the third thing likewise, Luke 10:33–34, *A Samaritan came near him . . . and bandaged his wounds, having poured oil and wine on them*. Boaz ordered his harvesters not to stop Ruth gleaning, but rather to be less careful themselves. And Christ orders the doctors not to stop scholars from making other expositions of Scripture, but rather He wishes that these doctors leave some parts unexpounded for the Minors to deal with.

The Lord be with you (Luke 1:28). These words of peace and salvation He at whose birth the angels sang *Glory to God in the highest* brought to His household.

May the Lord bless you. The crowd did well to shout to Him, Blessed is He who comes (Matt. 21:9).

Who does this girl belong to? Because Christ questioned any of the doctors who were in charge of the minor priests as if He were ignorant of the faith of the people, in order to challenge him to preach.

Early this morning: from the beginning of the faith right up to the completion of good works.

Stood in the field, persevering in the teaching of the preachers, so that she kept in her mind the words of salvation, the testimony of the Scriptures, and the example of the virtuous.

Gone home, to ancient superstition.

Hear me, daughter, that is, do not go back from the state of faith to heresies or schisms. Or, do not go to another faculty, namely civil or canon law (but few hear this voice).[36] Whence Hosea 8:12, *I have written for him the multitude of my law*. Again, Hosea 3:1, *Just as the Lord loves the people of Israel*. Again Hosea 9:1, *You have loved a prostitute's pay*.

Join my young girls: with the holy souls, because morals are formed by society. Bad company corrupts good morals (1 Cor. 5:9–11).

To my baggage. Hope that you will drink of the water of the knowledge of salvation (Ecclus 15:3), and draw divine wisdom from the rivers of the two Testaments.

And she, falling. The Church of the Gentiles gives thanks to the Savior who deigned to take care of her.

A foreign woman. Prov. 31:10, *A capable wife, who can find? She is far more precious than jewels.*

Abandoned your parents. She was glad because, since her husband was dead (that is, the devil and the world and its desires), she had given up her carnal desires so that she might be joined to the community of saints, of whom formerly she was ignorant.

Came to this people. Matt. 8:10, *I have found no such faith in Israel.*

Did not previously know. Ps. 18:43, *People whom I had not known, served me.*

For your deeds, and by faith: John 6:29, *This is the work of God.*

Receive full reward: eternal glory (John 16:24, *Ask and you will receive*).

Wings: the two testaments, by which God protects those who flee to Him. Ps. 57:1, *In the shadow of your wings*, and Matt. 23:37, *Jerusalem, Jerusalem, the city that kills the prophets and stones those who are sent to it.*

Come for refuge: consoling. Note that Boaz spoke to Ruth first.

Come for refuge: consoling her. Because God first leads the soul out of the state of sin, and then He speaks to the heart. Speaking, He inflames feelings with the fire of His love, and illuminates understanding with the light of His truth. Whence Hosea 2:14, *I will lead her into the wilderness.*

As though I were like. Behold the humility of the Gentile Church, who does not dare to equate herself to the early Church, but confesses herself inferior to such grace. Whence Matt. 15:27, *Even the dogs eat the crumbs*; and Matt. 8:8, *Lord, I am not worthy to have you come under my roof.*

When it is evening, which was when He said to the apostles, *Go and teach all the nations* (Matt. 28:19), to them He had earlier said, *Go nowhere among the Gentiles* (Matt. 10:5).

Eat the bread. Note that Boaz first gives Ruth permission to drink with his workers, and then he gives her permission to eat their bread. In the same way a doctor ought first to give the drink of Scripture, that is, to teach the simpler and easier parts, and afterwards he can minister the solid food, that is, the deeper and subtler parts, just as the Apostle did in 1 Cor. 3:1, *As infants in Christ.*

In the vinegar: in the Law which, having survived for a long time, corrupted by the traditions of the Pharisees, squanders its natural savor. In this the Church [dipped] a morsel that is the mystery of the incarnation of Christ, whom she recognized as long before having been prefigured and told of by the Old Testament, and therefore she believed more firmly.

And so she sat: because the Gentile Church united herself by faith to holy preachers.

Was satisfied, because knowledge of divine Law refreshes the devout mind.

And took the rest away. Remembering the individual words she had heard, she considered each with a subtle discretion.

It became the custom. She worked earnestly in meditation, so that she might understand greater things.

Throw out grain. Note the humility of the father of the household, who not only permitted the grains of teaching to be collected but even shared his sheaves of knowledge.

No-one should reprove her: because he did not despise the weakness of the Gentile people, nor linger on their original errors, but led them by wise study to edification.

Cutting and shaking out: because holy Church chooses the spiritual sense from the letter of the Law by the rod of discretion.[37]

Three measures: the faith of the Trinity, which preaches three persons in one divine substance.

Carrying this: because she showed her faith to Mother Church.

Or, the Church speaks to the Synagogue about faith, or about the grace which she received as a gift from her spouse, in order to challenge her to believe.

Gave her the rest: Ps. 45:1, *My heart overflows with a goodly word*, namely, the food of preaching from the fullness of the heart.

May he be blessed. The Gentile Church knew

the goodness and power of the Lord and the strength of His protection by the preaching of the Synagogue.

To the living: to the Jews who enjoyed His blessings.

To the dead: to the Gentiles who were buried in sin.

Our neighbor: said by the Synagogue according to the flesh; by the Church according to the Spirit.[38]

In another field: the doctrine of heretics or schismatics, where there are arguments and contention.

Barley: the letter of the Law, which was given to the Jews like pasture is given to a beast of burden.

Wheat: the grace of the New Testament, offered to reasonable people for food; [the wheat] in which the body and blood of Christ is offered (John 12:24, *Unless a grain of wheat*).

Until, that is, for as long as she stays with the doctors, she lays up knowledge of the Old and New Testaments in the cellars of her heart, whence she has food for the soul.

CHAPTER 3

I will try. The primitive Church took thought as to how the Gentile Church ought to come to union with Christ.

Threshing floor. Christ winnows the Synagogue in which the barley of the Law was stored up, preaching the Gospel in Judah and knowing the wills and plans each one had for themselves: John 2:24–25, *Jesus, however, knew what was in everyone.*

Wash yourself with the water of baptism or the tears of penitence.

Anoint yourself with the chrism or oil of the holy Spirit.

Put on your best clothes: the ornament of virtue.

The man may not see you, because the faith of the Gentile Church does not appear before Christ fulfills the mystery of the incarnation; but rather He went to His passion and resurrection after the meal with His disciples.

Eating and drinking, with the disciples: Heb. 2:14, *The lads shared the flesh and blood and he himself likewise partook with them.*

To go to sleep, that is, to die for us, through which all things are secured (John 12:32, *When I am lifted up from the earth*).

Turn back: As if to say, "Do you not know that Christ suffered for you," and "Smash the letter of the Old Testament in which the sacrament of the incarnation and passion lie hidden," and "Flee to him for help so that you might remain with him for all time."

He will tell you: because it is necessary that you learn the order of your salvation for yourself. Because the world has been entangled in the darkness of error, he shows us the swift faith of the Church for us to imitate. If, however, you transfer Naomi's words to the Synagogue [they mean]: [You may] discover in the Law and the prophets that the Gentile Church would come to the faith after the passion.

She did all. *Gloss*: The Church's obedience merits the fulfilment of her desires. Matt. 15:28, *Woman, great is your faith!*

Pile of hay: the witness of the Scriptures, or the crowds of the faithful whom he freed from hell. Matt. 26:24, *The Son of Man goes, as it is written of him.*

Woman: the Church.

Lying: humbly venerating the mystery of the incarnation.

Who are you? He asks for the Church's confession of faith.

Spread your blanket. She desires the protection and the grace of Christ, before all things.

You are blessed: because she has complete faith; as in Matt. 15:28, *Woman, great is your faith*; and she was worthy of His blessing and grace and virtue.

Former pity, by which [it means] taking thought for you, so that you abandon idolatry.

You have surpassed, because after you have come to Christ, you should persevere firmly in the faith.

Young men: heretics or schismatics, who do not have maturity of purpose, because they are always unstable and undecided.

I shall do for you. Luke 11:9, *Seek and you will find. Gloss:* whatever a faithful man rightly seeks, the kindness of Christ will give.

Everyone . . . knows you: because the faithful are firmly convinced that the Church is full of virtues. Prov. 31:10, *Who can find a capable wife?*

There is someone, that is, John the Baptist, who was thought to be Christ; but he did not usurp the name of the bridegroom, reserving that for Christ: John 3:29, *He who has the bride is the bridegroom.* He is the nearest relation because he was born first in this world. Or it means the ten commandments (which were specifically given to that people and at an earlier time), were closer to the Synagogue than the Gospel is.

Stay here tonight, until the darkness of unbelief lifted.

Before men: because before the Jews had been imbued with the teaching of the Law, they knew their own natural law. When the Gentile Church had been aroused from the sleep of ignorance, rising at the dawn of the birth of faith, she hastened to the grace of Christ.

Take care that you do not look for human praise of your conversation. Matt. 6:3, *When you give alms, do not let your left hand know what your right hand is doing.*

Stretch out, that is, spread your faith.

Both hands. Practice in your deeds what you have mercy on in your heart.

Six measures: because understanding is given according to capability, as much as one can take, so that everything is enriched with the divine gift. For the number six here can signify that the Lord gave the spiritual understanding of the barley of the Law to the Gentile Church in the sixth age.[39]

Carrying this: enriched by the blessing of Christ and adorned by the fruits of virtue.

And she told her the great things God has done, in order to call the primitive Church to praise and the Synagogue to conversion, which is her fellowship.

The man will not rest: because Christ took them from the prophecy of His incarnation to its fulfillment. Or [it means] He will not cease to fulfill what He promised when He said, *Whoever believes and is baptized will be saved* (Mark 16:16).

CHAPTER 4

Boaz went up, that is, Christ [went up to the gate], because, He took on flesh in the virgin's womb in which He showed Himself. About which gate Ezech. 44:2, *This gate shall remain shut . . . for the Lord, the God of Israel, has entered by it.*

And when he saw. Christ made the Law handed down to the Jews pause to witness to the mystery of His stewardship. Or, "he saw the closer relative go past" means He saw His precursor's coming hastened by the way they were leading their lives, and He turned with pity to the duty of preaching.

Calling his name John, through Gabriel (Luke 1:13).

Ten men, fathers of the Old Testament, who by keeping the ten commandments, understood that the incarnation of Christ was prefigured in the Law.

Part of the field. *Gloss:* he offered part of Naomi's field for purchase, in a way suitable to the legislators, since grace apparently remained for saving part of the people; He showed it to the masters of the Synagogue so that they knew their weakness; and because they could not [help] themselves, they entrusted themselves to the help of a true doctor. Whence it is said to the lepers, *Go and show yourselves* (Luke 17:14).

To keep alive. This signifies no other possession of the people than the union of the Church in marriage with Christ, who revives the ancient name of "sons of God," which the saints had in the beginning (Gen. 6:2, 4, *The sons of God*; and Lk 3:38, *Son of Adam, son of God*), whom Christ revived in the Gentile Church through grace (John 1:12, *He gave power to become children of God*). The ten commandments could not revive this name among the nations. If you would rather think to give this name to John the Baptist, he himself gave it away by the right of the closer relative: John 1:26, *I baptize you with water* etc.; and John 3:28, *I am not the Christ*. So too, the Law gives way to the Gospel. For the Law came about so that wrong might abound; but when wrong abounds then grace superabounds (Rom. 5:20). *There was the abrogation of an earlier commandment*, Heb. 7:18.

The man undid his own sandal. The sandal is the veil of mysteries which the Law gave to Christ, because the Law could not make manifest the sacraments through the teachers of the people; but that was kept for Christ to do. Therefore John lays claim to the sandal not for himself but for Christ, because he understood the spouse to belong to Christ alone.

As witnesses. Christ has sufficient witnesses from both Testaments and peoples because the Gentile people (whom the commandments, which were already spiritually at an end, could not make frutiful) possessed all things which the earlier and later saints had, who could themselves fertilize [others] with the seed of the Word.

And the elders. Isidore: the blessing of the ten elders shows that all people are blessed in the name of Jesus. For iota, which is the first letter in the name of Jesus, signifies ten in Greek.

Rachel: a type of internal contemplation, having a sure understanding of truth. And a studious man loves all pious women, because a beautiful woman belongs to this type. And on account of this, that is, the grace of God, through which we are made white (Isai. 1:18, *Though your sins are scarlet, they shall be white as snow*), Laban kept her back.

Leah. Leah signifies the deeds of this life in which we live, struggling with faith, and uncertain of how things may turn out for the good of those we wish to look after. The primitive Church prays for the abundance of their prosperity with the Gentile Church.

Perez. He is a type of the Gentile people because it was he who first set the Jewish hand to the works of the Law; and afterwards he drew back, defiled by the blood of Christ, and of the prophets; by birth, he took precedence (Gen. 38:28–30). *So the first shall be last and the last first*, Matt. 20:16.

Tamar is interpreted as "changing" or "bitterness." She is the Gentile Church, who changed her name and appearance. For she was filthy and bitter in idolatry, and sweet and beautiful in penitence.

Made her conceive: because with Christ, the Church brought forth every spiritual child. Whence 1 Sam. 2:5, *The barren woman has borne many children*.

Blessed be the Lord. The Church is continually made fruitful by the grace of the holy Spirit; and as some pass into perpetual light, others succeed them; so that the name of Christ continues in perpetuity, and holy Mother [Church] is consoled in her old age by her new children. And so the apostles and evangelists succeed to the patriarchs and prophets who pass away (Ps. 45:16, *In the place of ancestors, you shall have sons*).

From your daughter-in-law. Synagogue is the mother-in-law of the Church who married Christ, who was himself born from the Synagogue.

As his nurse. She who was not able to have children of her own (from the Law), carried the mystery received through the prophets, hidden under the veil of figures; and she did this through the office of nursemaid, because she did not have the privileges of a mother.

The neighborhood women congratulated her: the virtuous people of heaven praising the fertility of the Church.

<u>They named him Obed</u>, that is, "serving." They desire to serve with the heavenly king.

<u>Jesse fathered David</u>. The spiritual lineage is woven here. Obed, "serving," Isaiah, "sacrifice" or "incense," David, "strong of hand" or "desirable." For whoever serves God strenuously offers thanks and sweet incense to him, that is, works of virtue and prayer. And so, invigorated by faith and devotion, they desire to please God.

<u>These are the generations</u>. Note that there are ten generations of sons of Judah up to David, because the intention of the whole Law leans towards Christ, born from the seed of David (Rom. 10:4, *Christ is the end of the Law*; Gen. 49:10, *The scepter shall not depart from Judah*). And about David, born from the tribe of Judah: *One of the sons of your body I will set on your throne* (Ps. 132:11). Therefore it is clear that the prophecies of all the prophets and patriarchs refer to our Lord Jesus Christ. Amen.

Translated from the Paris, 1533, edition of Hugh's *Postillae*.

Notes

1. Rashi on Ruth, Breithaupt, p. 104.

2. Peter Comestor in the *Scholastic History* (*Historia scholastica*), quoting Rabanus Maurus on Ruth.

3. See Introduction. In fact, as we have noted, Ruth's position was moveable, sometimes at the end of Judges, more often with the Megillot, in liturgical order.

4. Hugh uses *Solutio* here as though he were answering a scholastic question in the middle of the exegesis. This habit can also be seen in Stephen Langton.

5. For the four women sinners, see Introduction.

6. Hugh is here employing a conventional *accessus*, in fashion at the time. He asks and answers (some) of the Aristotelian questions surrounding the "circumstances" of an act: "who?," "what?," "where?," "when?," "why?," "for whom?," "how?";

and he links them with the four "causes" of any creation: efficient (the author), material (his sources or intention), formal (his method), and final (always our salvation, for a Christian work). See A. J. Minnis, *Medieval Theory of Authorship: Scholastic Literary Attitudes in the Later Middle Ages* (Philadelphia, 1988), chapters 1 and 2.

7. Most of the Gloss was taken from Rabanus, as we have seen.

8. Rashi on Ruth, Breithaupt, p. 104.

9. This interpretation suggests that there is no "historical" sense for the famine, i.e., that it never actually happened. He may think Peter Comestor is wrong not to have an historical interpretation but he does not himself talk about a "real" famine. It also suggests a disapproval of spiritual men involving themselves in politics or secular power.

10. Jerome, *Liber de nominibus Hebraicis*, PL 23:809–10; ibid., *Liber de situ et nominibus locorum Hebraicorum*, PL 23:879.

11. Jerome, *Quaestiones Hebraicae in . . . Paralipomenon*, PL 23:1373.

12. Lit. "a woman's things."

13. Lit. "seed."

14. What constituted a legal marriage was debated by medieval theologians. There were two main schools of thought. Gratian's *Decretum* and the canon lawyers held that both consent and consummation were necessary. Peter Lombard's *Sentences* required only consent, but it must be in the present, not the future. "Medieval canon law inherited the rules of Roman law, that no betrothal might be undertaken under seven, and that the age of consent was the age of puberty, deemed to be twelve for a girl, fourteen for a boy"; see C. N. L. Brooke, *The Medieval Idea of Marriage* (Oxford and New York, 1991), p. 138, n. 44.

15. Rabanus Maurus on Ruth, *PL* 108:1203C.

16. Rashi on Ruth, Breithaupt, p. 109.

17. I.e., there are two readings of the text, "your husband" or "her husband." Both are possible, as both were dead.

18. *Affca* is in fact the Hebrew word for powder.

19. This is one of a number of occasions where Hugh takes a

rather syntactical approach to the text, taking pains with the meaning of individual words and phrases, as part of his literal interpretation.

20. Cf. *Historia scholastica* at this point.

21. Hugh is explaining the rather unusual word *archonius*. The printed text reads *immolatus in summo acutus*, which makes no sense here. I have amended to *immolitus*.

22. In fact, in the Jerome text, he is called "brother." Hugh has a slightly different version of the Bible. See L. Light, *French Bibles ca. 1200–1300: A New Look at the Origin of the Paris Bible*, in R. Gameson, ed., *The Early Medieval Bible* (Cambridge, 1994), pp. 155–76.

23. This legal note is reminiscent of privileges given to crusaders. The well-used privilege given in *Quantum praedecessores* of Eugenius III, in 1145, allowed land to be used as security in loans for those going on crusade, and assumed that the landholder would first ask his relatives or fiefholders to lend him the money, using the land as a pledge. See J. A. Brundage, *Medieval Canon Law and the Crusader* (Madison, Wis., 1969), pp. 175–76. Compare also the preferential options for purchase and use of land in the contract made by Hugues and Garin de Chilley with the monastery of Our Lady of Ferté, printed in G. Duby, *Rural Economy and Country Life in the Medieval West*, trans. C. Postan (Columbia, S.C., 1968), no. 121, pp. 475–76. I am grateful to Dr. Jean Dunbabin for this suggestion.

24. Josephus, *Antiquities*, bk 5, c. 9.

25. Hugh does not fill in all the possible cases here, perhaps because it is too complicated.

26. Hugh implies here that Boaz was saving the unnamed relative from disgrace by allowing him the opportunity to remove his own sandal, rather than having it taken from him.

27. Ps.-Chrysostom, *Opus Imperfectum*, PG 56:620.

28. Rabanus Maurus on Ruth, quoted in the Gloss.

29. *Peregrinatio* is used to mean both pilgrimage and exile here.

30. This is something of a play on words, since *liberi* can mean both "children" and "free men" in Latin.

31. The Chapter of a cathedral or monastic community is the collective membership responsible for its government.

32. This little simile seems to refer to little more than lions as wild animals, although in medieval bestiaries lions could sometimes symbolize the devil. However, medieval images are always more fluid and polysemous than modern minds may find comfortable. Lions, for instance, were also very often symbolic of Christ, since they were believed to give birth to their young stillborn, and lick them in to life three days later.

33. This replacement of "son" by "nephew" is a joke, reminding readers that the illegitimate children of clergy were often termed their nieces and nephews.

34. Note the altered allegorical interpretation of Naomi who, instead of being simply the Synagogue, has become those first Jews who turned to Christ—the primitive Church.

35. The barley harvest would have happened in late April and May. This is about the same time as the feast of Weeks, with which Ruth is associated in the Megillot.

36. In most medieval universities or *studia generales* there were four faculties of higher study: theology, medicine, canon law, and civil law. Particular universities were generally famous for one of these. Paris was renowned across Europe for theology. In 1219, Honorius III banned the study of Roman (civil) law at Paris, probably at the request of Philip II, who did not want Roman law principles to interfere with the customary law of France. Since civil law was a prerequisite for canon law, Paris never grew to importance in legal study. Then, as now, qualifying in law was a passport to a good salary, and this stood in contrast to the mendicancy (that is, voluntary poverty) of the Dominicans whom Hugh was teaching.

37. Medieval exegetes were careful not to make a simple distinction between the Old Law and the New Covenant in terms of the latter superseding the former. Instead, they explained Paul's "the letter kills but the spirit gives life" (2 Cor. 3: 6) to mean that both Old and New could contain both letter and spirit, depending upon their interpretation. In this way they avoided the Marcionite heresy (repeated by Manicheans) which held the Old Testament, and everything contained in it, was useless—and indeed wrong—to Christians, who had been given the Gospel and holy Spirit.

38. Hugh is saying that the Jews mean this in the literal sense, to say that he was a good man, but Christians mean it in a mystical sense, to say that Christ was truly human.

39. For the six ages see n. 4, p. 25.

Nicholas of Lyra: Postills on Ruth

The Literal Sense

CHAPTER 1

<u>In the days</u>. Here follows the third case, namely, that of Ruth.[1] And it is divided into four parts, since first it tells of Ruth's gracious conversion, second, of her virtuous conversation, third, of the legal convention, and fourth, of her marriage; each part beginning in each of the four chapters of this story. The first part has two sections, the occasion of her conversion and, second, the conversion itself, beginning at *Naomi said to her*. In fact, the occasion of Ruth's conversion to Judaism was that she was married to the son of Elimelech, who was exiled from Judah in the land of Moab. And so Elimelech's exile is described first of all, and, second, Ruth's marriage, beginning at *They took*. Concerning the first of these, the time of the exile is described first, when it says:

<u>In the days of a certain judge</u>. Who this was, however, is variously explained. For the Master of the Histories[2] and other expositors say that he was the judge Eli, who usurped the priesthood because he was not from the line of Eleazar but of Ithamar. However, although this second thing is true as far as it goes, because Eli was *not* from the line of Eleazar but of Ithamar, yet it does not seem true that he usurped the priesthood, because in 1 Sam. 2:30, the Lord in person says to Eli, *I promised that your family and the family of your ancestors should go in and out before me forever* etc. From which it is seen that his priesthood was held by divine ordination, as is said in the same place more fully.

The first thing said, then, seems not to be true, namely, that Elimelech's exile (which is described here), happened at the time of Eli, because from the time at which he began to judge Israel to the beginning of the reign of David, eighty years passed, according to what is declared earlier in Judges 11. During this time, therefore, the second thing spoken of happened, that is, Elimelech's exile and Boaz's fathering of Obed with Ruth, and Obed fathering Jesse, and Jesse David, and David's life up to the beginning of his reign. This does not seem to be true. First, because at least eleven years passed between that time and Obed's birth, that is, ten years when Naomi stayed in Moab, and this chapter is set one year before the birth of Obed (because Boaz took Ruth as his wife immediately after her arrival in Bethlehem). So, eleven years had passed in total, or at all events approximately that number, before Obed was born.

Again, David lived for thirty years before he began to rule, as it says in 2 Sam. 5:4. Again, David's father Jesse was already an old man when he fathered David, it would seem, because he already had six sons (as it says in 1 Sam. 16:10 *et seq.*, and 1 Chron. 2:13–16[3]), and so it seems that he was at least thirty-nine years old when he fathered David. Indeed, this is clear from 1 Sam. 17:12, which says that he was an old man of many years; indeed, he was a veteran of the army when David, as a youth, was sent to visit his brothers. So then if these years are added up they make eighty years, and no time is left over for Obed's life, for him to be able to father Jesse. (Indeed, I assume in saying this that Elimelech began his exile in the first year Eli ruled.) So that it does not seem to be true that Ruth's story happened in the time of Eli, but before that. And therefore the Hebrews say something else—and better, it would seem—that the judge here was Abesan, of whom Judges 12:1

speaks, who judged forty-seven years before Eli, as is clear from Judges 11. Indeed, the Hebrews say that this Abesan and Boaz were the same person with two names. Following this line, one must still say that Elimelech's exile began before Boaz began to rule, because he judged the people for only seven years, and Naomi was in Moab ten years, as it says earlier in the same chapter, and Boaz took Ruth as his wife after that. Nevertheless, the exile up to Naomi's return was finished under Abesan, who is the same person as Boaz according to the Hebrews. Therefore they call this his [Abesan's] time, because a thing is named after its end. And so this story is placed here (in the list of judges) to show how king David was descended from Boaz, as is clear at the end.

There was a famine, on account of the sins of the people.

A man went out from Bethlehem. The cause of this exile is explained in various ways. For Jerome said (about the fourth chapter of Chronicles[4]) that at that time the sun stopped moving across the sky, to make men afraid, so that they would turn away from the grave sins in which they were entangled. But they did not do this; and for this reason such a great famine occurred in the land that Elimelech, who was from the nobler and more powerful town of Bethlehem, was compelled to go to a foreign land to make a living. The Hebrews, however, say that because of the famine in the land many poor people turned to Elimelech, who was rich and powerful, and he was harsh towards them because of his avarice; and so he left the land of Israel with all the goods he could carry, to avoid their begging. And because he left for a bad motive, he died there with his sons and was impoverished. The rest is clear in the literal sense.

Who took wives. After this, Ruth's marriage is described. The Hebrews (and even certain Catholics) say that this Ruth was the daughter of Eglon, the king of Moab. But this seems to be untrue, because from the time of Ehud, who killed Eglon (as Judges 3:12–26 says), up to Abesan, thirty-two

years passed (as Judges 12[5] says), and there were many more years until Eli; and so, if Abesan was the same person as Boaz, as the Hebrews say, it is impossible that Ruth was the daughter of Eglon, whom Ehud killed, because she was still young enough to have children when she was married to Boaz.[6] Again, if Boaz was someone other than Abesan, then because Ruth's story happened at the time of Eli, as others say, it is even more impossible that Ruth was the daughter of the aforesaid Eglon, because there were many more years till the time of Eli than to the time of Abesan, as Judges 12 declares.

And therefore if anyone wishes to say that Ruth was the daughter of Eglon the king of Moab, they must say that this Eglon was someone other than the Eglon whom Ehud killed, and who lived a long time after him. But indeed, it does not then seem consistent with what the Hebrews and the Catholics who follow Jerome say, that Elimelech was a poor man when he was in Moab. And according to the Hebrews although he was wealthy in Judah, in Moab he was impoverished, as was said above. And so it seems from this (as is said in the same chapter), that Naomi returned from Moab with nothing, that is, without a husband, sons or wealth. But it is not true that the king of Moab would give his daughter to a poor man and an outsider, to be his wife; and if her husband became impoverished after the giving, it is not true that he would permit her to leave her own land as a pauper who needed to glean grain in a stranger's field, as is said of Ruth later. And therefore it rather seems that Ruth was of humble origins herself.

For she had heard. And so, because the famine had left her own land, she was better able to return to it.

Go home to your mothers. She said this because their fathers were dead or because women are closer to their mothers than to their fathers.

Who, raising their voices, lamented. From which it is clear that Naomi was very close to her daughters-in-law.

I have no other sons. For there was a precept of

the Law (Deut. 25:5–10) that if anyone died without heirs, leaving a wife, his brother should take her as his wife, in order to revive the name[7] of his dead brother. The rest is clear in the literal sense.

To whom she said. After this, Ruth's conversion is described. She did not wish to return home, as the other daughter-in-law did, and she converted to the worship of the one God, leaving behind her Gentile identity. And on account of this it says: Do not . . . make me leave you, turning back to the worship of idols.

Wherever. Here the Hebrews say that willing converts to the God of Judaism must be told the most difficult parts of the Law, at least in part, in the same way as the difficulties of this religion must be explained to those wishing to enter into it.[8] Therefore, they say that Naomi, seeing Ruth wish to convert to Judaism, told her some of the burdens of the Law. And first she told her that it was not lawful for Jews to go outside the land of Israel, except in great necessity. And then Ruth answered her "*Wherever you go, I shall go*, and nowhere else." Again, she said to her, "It is not lawful among us for a woman to be alone with a man, unless he is her husband" and Ruth answered "*Wherever you lodge, I shall lodge*, unwilling to be with another man without you." Again, she said "The Hebrew people is subject to the burdens of the Law, in which there are six hundred and thirteen precepts." Then she answered, *Your people are my people*, which is to say "I wish to be subject to that Law." Again, she said, "It is forbidden to us to worship other gods." And she answered, *Your God is my God*, which is to say "I do not wish to worship any other god." Again she said to her, "In some cases a fourfold penalty of death (by stoning, burning, strangulation by hanging, or death by the sword) is imposed on transgressors of our Law, as is clear in Exodus and Deuteronomy."[9] And then Ruth answered, *Whichever land takes you at death, there shall I die*, which is to say, "I am prepared to receive whatever death penalty I should merit, just like you."

Therefore, seeing. Because when anyone has made up their mind to turn to the divine Law or religion, they must not be checked or impeded. The rest is clear up to here.

The women said. According to our expositors, this should be read with the voice turned down (*depressive*), as in a statement, and it is said in rejoicing at the return of Naomi. According to the Hebrews,[10] however, it is read with the voice turned up, (*interrogative*), as in a question, and it is said in wonder, as if they said, "*This* is Naomi?," who left with a wagon and horses and riches, and comes back like this, a pauper, on foot, because she left the land of Israel for bad reasons, as was said earlier, according to the Hebrew belief. And this is consonant with what follows.

I set out with sons and riches.

Empty. And in this she confessed the punishment inflicted on her by God for her sin in leaving the land of Israel for a bad reason, as was said earlier according to Hebrew belief.

CHAPTER 2

There was a kinsman. Ruth's virtuous conversation is described in what follows. And because humility is the foundation of all virtue, therefore what is first described about her is her virtue of humility; second is the ornament of her honesty (at *It happened, however*); the third virtue is her gratitude for kindness (at *Accordingly, she collected*). Her humility is apparent in that she debased herself so far as to glean grain in a field, following the wish and desire of her mother-in-law. The name of Boaz (in whose field she gleaned), precedes hers, however, [in the text] because he was a kinsman of her dead husband, and this is what is said:

There was a kinsman. The Hebrews say that Elimelech, Ruth's father-in-law, and Salmon, Boaz's father, were brothers, and so Ruth's husband and Boaz were closely related by blood.[11] But it seems that the first statement is untrue, because Salmon, who fathered Boaz with Rahab, was alive at the time of Joshua, and took Rahab as his wife after the destruction of Jericho, because she joined the people of Israel at that time, as it says in Joshua 6. However, this was about the beginning of Joshua's leadership. And indeed, from the beginning of his leadership up to the time of Abesan (whom the Hebrews say was Boaz himself), was two hundred and seventy two years, and even more years passed until the time of Eli. Therefore, if we may say, following the opinion of the Hebrews, that Boaz and Abesan were the same person, then it seems impossible that Elimelech was Salmon's brother because Ruth (who was the wife of Maalon, Elimelech's son), was a young girl at that time, as is clear enough from what follows (that when she married Boaz, she was old enough to bear children). If we were to say that Boaz was of the same generation as Eli, who ruled for many years afterwards, that would be impossible. Because of this, our doctors say (and rightly, it seems), that there were three Boazes successively, of which the first was the uncle, the second the son, and the third the nephew. The first was the son of Salmon, whom he fathered with Rahab, and the third was he who fathered Obed with Ruth. And this is the same one referred to in Matthew, chapter 1, where these three are conflated under one name, because the Evangelist Matthew wished to describe the genealogy of the Savior in three lots of fourteen ancestors, as is said afterwards in the same place,[12] in which order the third Boaz is the one pertaining to Elimelech himself and to his son Maalon. The rest is clear in the literal sense.

It happened, however. Here is the ornament of honesty described in Ruth. Boaz perceived this, visiting his harvesters. And so the text adds:
And he said etc. According to what the Hebrews say,[13] and it is apparent enough from the text, Boaz was already a man of advanced age, and an honorable one by reason of his knowledge and virtue; and therefore, it is not true that he was looking for some young girl for a wife, unless he saw in her a singular honesty; and therefore the Hebrews say

that she collected the grain which remained standing after the harvesters had done their work standing up, but she collected the grain lying on the field sitting down, in case her clothes might be lifted up at the back and her thighs might be uncovered when she bent down to gather it.[14]

Therefore Boaz, seeing her honesty, was moved to ask who she was and to be kind towards her, saying to her what follows:
Hear me, daughter. The literal sense is clear. It is certainly clear that she was a young girl in comparison to him, because he called her "daughter."

Who, falling. Here Ruth is commended in gratitude for, having shown kindnesses to Boaz, although they were not very big things, she was greatly repaid for them; and the literal sense is clear up to here.

I am not. In Hebrew it says "of your maidservants," which is to say "I am not as worthy as the least of your maidservants," and therefore Boaz wins greater thanks for himself. Whence it follows:
And he said, etc., that is, food prepared in my house with my household.

And dip. For vinegar is very cooling, and therefore in hot regions, of the sort that the land of Israel is, it is drunk at times of great heat, such as harvest.[15]

And she ate, that is, Ruth prepared her food herself, according to our translation. In Hebrew it says "Food was prepared for her," that is, food was made from new grain, which Boaz gave Ruth with his own hand, as the Hebrews say. The rest is clear in the literal sense.

Accordingly, she collected. In what follows, Ruth's carefulness in the work which she had come to do (following her mother-in-law's wish) is described, when it is said:
Accordingly, she collected. However, the addition "that is, three" is not in the Hebrew, which instead has "of barley," because she found an ephah of barley in what she had collected. However, the measure of this amount was an ephah, as was said in Exodus 16. For a gomor was a tenth part of an

ephah and a gomor of manna was sufficient for one day for one person, as is said in the same place.

She joined herself, that is, to the maidservants. The rest is clear in the literal sense.

CHAPTER 3

When, however. Following this, the legal convention with regard to Ruth is described because, in accordance with the Law about the reviving of the name of the dead (as Deut. 25 has it), she herself sought marriage from Boaz, following her mother-in-law's plan. And so, first comes her mother-in-law's plan, second the daughter-in-law's obedience, and third is the reasonable response by Boaz. The second part starts at *And she answered*, the third at *You are blessed*. About the first part, it is said:

When, however, that is, after the harvesting, when she was joined up with Boaz's girls, as was said earlier, at the end of chapter 2.

I will try to get you rest, that is, a good marriage, so that you might not have to work for a living.

And provide for you having children, which women most want to do.

And tonight he winnows, that is, he made a holiday of the winnowing. For certain people say it was the custom of the ancients to have a feast for the winnowers at the winnowing of the grain, and to sleep the night on the threshing floor. Rashi[16] says about this that at that time there were many thieves in the land, and so Boaz went there to sleep because, in his presence, the winnowed grain might be better guarded by his servants; and both of these could be the reason for doing it.

Wash. She said this so that Boaz might be more inclined to marry her.

The man, namely, Boaz himself.

Until he has finished eating and drinking. She said this because it was then that men were more likely to contract and consummate marriage. On this point, some people say that Naomi had not sinned herself, because she was seeking to revive the name of the dead man through the law of matrimony. However, the opposite seems rather to be true, because the method of looking for a husband here was not a good one (that is to say, in the dark), and also because there was a closer relative than Boaz, who ought to have been the first to be asked (as is explained later), and so someone would be hard done by unless he voluntarily ceded his rights in Law. It is on account of all this that Boaz told Ruth that she should conceal what she did. Ruth however, who was newly converted to Judaism and did not know what the Law about matrimony required, nor about the means of going about it, except for what her mother-in-law taught her, was totally excused.

And she answered. After this Ruth's obedience is described, because she did everything her mother-in-law said, believing that she acted well in everything. And the literal sense is clear up to here.

The man was afraid. Rashi says that he feared that it was an evil spirit which might be taken into his body from his feet up, or that perhaps he feared robbers.[17]

And was perturbed. The Hebrew says, "And he feared" or, "he embraced," because he stretched out his hand and touched Ruth's head and knew by this that she was a woman, because women have heads which feel different from men's heads, and which are covered.[18] Therefore it is added:

And he saw the woman, that is, he knew by touching. He could not know by sight because it was night. But the word "see" is sometimes used for one of the other senses, as in Exodus 20:18, The whole people saw voices, that is, they heard them. However, Boaz did not know then what the woman intended, so he asked, *Who are you?*

Spread your blanket follows. With this phrase she was asking to be betrothed to him.[19] For this was the custom at the time, that the bridegroom contracted an engagement by placing the corner of his cloak over his bride-to-be. However, other people say that by this favor (*curialiter*) she sought the consummation of marriage, following what her mother-in-law had taught her. Boaz held her to be completely blameless for this reason, because the Hebrews say that Ruth spoke to Boaz first,[20] following what her mother-in-law had taught her, saying, "My mother-in-law and I need to sell the inheritance which came from Elimelech and his sons, and you are the kinsman who may redeem it, as it says in Levit. 25:25. So take up the inheritance, and me along with it, as your wife, in order to revive the name of the dead man in his children."

Because "You are the nearest relative, on whom the redemption of the inheritance and the reviving of his name relies" (according to the double law already mentioned). And this speech is consonant with what Boaz said, *Naomi is selling part of a field*.

And he. Following this, Boaz made a reasonable response[21] and sent her out again with kindness (at *And she arose*). About the first part it is said:

You are blessed. And this shows that she was blameless, for the reason already explained; and with this he showed good will towards her, saying:

And your former pity. He called the first thing pity because she had behaved so well towards her husband when he lived, and towards her mother-in-law (which Boaz had heard of from stories about her), as was said earlier, in chapter 2. The second "pity" he spoke of, however, is the will she had to restore the name of the dead man through marriage; and he calls this greater than the first because it is the greater mercy to do good for someone after his death when he is not able to help himself, than while he lives. And he shows that Ruth herself was moved by love for a child, and not for love of lust, saying:

Because you have not run after young men, seeking to be joined with them in marriage; but I am an old man, in whose bed there is not such delight!

Do not be afraid. I will marry you.

Knows you, which is to say, I am prepared to take you as my wife because of your reputation for goodness; but I cannot do this lawfully unless he who is a closer kinsman gives up his rights in the matter. Therefore it is added:

But there is another, a closer relation, whose name is not given because he does not wish to revive his dead brother's name; and on account of this he is unworthy to be named. For Elimelech, Naomi's husband, and this Boaz's father, were brothers; and so another man was a closer kinsman by one degree.[22]

And she slept. And the continence of both of them is clear from this.

And she arose. After this, Ruth's gracious going out or sending out is described, first of all from Ruth's point of view, when it says:

Before. For she did not wish to be seen by men when she was leaving, in case an evil rumor was started about her and Boaz. Second, her leaving is described from Boaz's point of view, for he warns her about guarding their respective reputations, saying:

Take care. And because he did not want to send her back empty-handed, it adds:

Measures. The Hebrew has six measures of barley, but how big the measures were is not explained.[23] However, it seems from the circumstances of the text that they were not very great because they could be contained in Ruth's cloak, and because she could carry the whole thing herself on her head, back to town and to Naomi's house. Rashi says here that these six measures were a sign and a prefiguring of the six blessings of God upon the birth of the Messiah who was to come from Ruth through David and the royal genealogy, in accordance with what is said in Isai. 11:1–2, *A shoot shall come out*, and following, *And the fear of the Lord shall rest on him*. Our translation adds "and of piety," but it is not so in Hebrew. And from this statement of Rashi[24] we see two things: first, that the Old Testament writings must not only be interpreted *historically* but sometimes even *mysti-*

cally;[25] and second, that the saying of Isaiah previously mentioned is understood as being about Christ, even in Hebrew. The rest is clear in the literal sense.

CHAPTER 4

Boaz went up. Here finally, following the renunciation of his rights by the closer relative, Boaz and Ruth's marriage is described. And concerning this, first the summoning of the said relative is touched on, then the taking of Ruth as wife (at *And he said, before the elders*), third, the conception of the child (at *And he went in to her*), and fourth, the congratulations of the people (at *And the women said*). The first is in two parts, because first the summoning of the closer relative is described, then the giving-up of his right (at *To which he replied*). About the first part it says: He went up. For in former times judgements were held at the gate of the city, so that the place of justice might be open to everyone, quickly and easily.

And he sat as if he were the principal judge, in accordance with the Hebrews who say that he was Abesan himself, as was said above, in chapter 1.

Pause a little, so that you may answer in the place of judgement.

Bringing over, so that the contract might be agreed.

Part of the field. He calls him brother because he was a relative, and this way of speaking is frequent in scripture.

Naomi is selling, that is, "is proposing to sell," because the field had not been sold, as is made clear in what follows. The Hebrews however, do not have a present tense in the indicative mood of verbs, but use instead a present participle of time, commonly speaking, "selling" for "he sells," and sometimes [they use] the past tense of a verb in the indicative mood, as in this case. Or perhaps she had already sold it, and what the text adds about the purchase through the closest kinsman must be understood as the redemption of the purchase, which depends on the law of propinquity, as Lev. 25 says. It should be known, however, that although women could not inherit, nevertheless, a wife who was left without children after her husband's death could keep part of the inheritance during her lifetime, and she could sell as much of it as was her right. And so it says here that Naomi wanted to sell part of a field in that way. The rest is clear up to here.

No nearer relative. It must not be thought that she had no other relatives, since they were great and powerful men, but, because no-one was a closer relative than these two, there was no-one who had any rights in the contract.

Whereupon he replied. He very much wanted to have the land, but not the wife. However, one was a corollary of the other, and so it goes on: When you buy. And the literal sense is clear.

To which he replied. Following this, the giving-up of the right is described, when it says: I cede my right, for his reason is given when it says:
Nor can I, which some Hebrews interpret as being about the children and successors who would be born from Ruth if he took her as his wife, about which it is written in Deut. 23:3, *No Moabite or Ammonite shall be admitted to the assembly of the Lord.*[26] But if they give this as his reason they speak a falsehood, because that punishment does not fall on women nor, in accordance with that, on children born of an Israelite man, as was said in the same place.[27] And therefore this passage is explained another way, namely by the children he already had with another wife; since if he took Ruth as his wife he would have to look after the education of the children born from her and make provision for them, and consequently he would be less able to make provision for the children which he had from the other woman. And that is called *destruction* in common parlance, whereby it is said of anyone if he has some particular loss, that he is destroyed or wiped out.

The man undid his sandal: The man. This was

a sign that one man is unloosened from the Law, and the other is tied to it. Deut. 25:9, however, describes how the wife of a dead man loosened the sandal and spat in the face of the man who was unwilling to revive the dead man's name. But this was when the woman was present, together with him, in front of the judges, and he refused to take her as his wife. But when another relative joined them, just as is described here, then the man himself loosened his sandal; and so it adds *Boaz therefore said to his neighbor*.

And he said. After this the acceptance of the wife is described, when Boaz says for greater solemnity:

You are witnesses. For Boaz said this to the elders to certify the deed.

The Lord made this woman. Because her sons were made the heads of the twelve tribes of Israel; because she was the first and principal wife of Jacob, as Gen. 29 says; and because the agreement was first made about her, even though the other was fraudulently substituted for her, Rachel is placed above Leah, even though she was the younger.

May your house be established. This is said because the genealogy of David himself begins at Perez, when it is said, *These are the generations*.

And so Boaz took Ruth. It would seem that he acted against the Lord's prohibition about taking foreign wives (as Deut. 7:2–3 says). It must be said that the prohibition was made in case Israel fall into idolatry through foreign women. Ruth, however, had already converted to the faith and worship of the one God and was supported in this by her good life, as is clear from what has been said, and so the prohibition has no place here. But Maalon and Chilion do not seem able to be excused from this transgression, because they took Moabite wives before they were converted to the faith and worship of the one God, which is seen in this, that Orpha returned to her own gods (as was said above, chapter 1); and in this, that Naomi tried to persuade Ruth also to go back, which she would

not have done if she had converted already, because she would not have persuaded her to apostasize from the faith and worship of the one true God.

He went in. After this, the conception of the child is described, when it is said:

The Lord made her conceive. From which it would seem that she conceived so quickly by a man already aged, not only by virtue of nature but because nature was being aided by grace. And this was granted by God, because Boaz accepted Ruth out of fraternal charity to revive the name of the dead in his own children, and from obedience to the Law which Deut. 25 establishes.

The women said. After this, the people's congratulations are described, and the giving of thanks, when they say, *Blessed be the Lord* etc.

They named him Obed, because a son born this way was known as the son of the dead man, although he might be called by another name, as indeed he was called Obed, not Elimelech or Maalon.

He is far better. The congratulations to Naomi are exaggerated. Or perhaps it was better to have one nephew with a wealthy and powerful father than to have seven sons from a pauper, as Elimelech had been in the end (as was said earlier, chapter 1). The rest is clear in the literal sense.

Salmon was the father. There were three Boazes succeeding him, here subsumed under the same name, as was said earlier in chapter 2.

The Moral Sense

CHAPTER 1

A man went out. According to the Jews he was very wealthy, but miserly. Because of his wealth, at the time of famine annoying petitions were raised by his relatives and fellow-citizens who, driven by hunger, appealed for his help; and so, to get away from their solicitations, he left for the land of Moab, with his wife and sons and all the goods they could carry. And since he had a bad motive for leaving, the Lord punished him by his own death and that of his sons, and took away all his earthly goods; so that when she returned to Bethlehem his wife, Naomi, said, *I set out full*, as was said above.

The wealthy people of this world have a lesson in this, that they should not receive the petitions of the poor with annoyance, nor should they turn away from them without cause, lest they be punished as Elimelech was. As it says in Wisdom 11:16, *By whatever anyone sins, by this is he punished*; and Prov. 21:13, *If you close your ear to the cry of the poor*; and, for example, Luke 16:19–25, about the rich man at the banquet who could not get a drop of water because he refused a crumb of bread to Lazarus. How much more should they who are miserly with their knowledge, which is not diminished by sharing but increased, be afraid for themselves; and similarly for men wise about earthly matters, if they are greedy of giving counsel to the poor, where possession is not given over but only words. Ruth, however, when she left the Gentile people, stayed close to Naomi, saying: <u>Your God</u>. And she was indeed humbly obedient to her. She signifies the true penitent who, having left the slavery of the devil, stays close to the Church, humbly obeying her commandments. The Church is well-signified by "Naomi" which, for that reason, is interpreted as meaning "beautiful." And Song 4:1 says about the Church, *How beautiful you are, my love*. And so it was in the beginning, but now it [the Church] can say, *Call me not Naomi*. For there are many who live off the goods of the Church lavishly and magnificently, and they incite much bitterness by their evil lives. Blessed Bernard, speaking in person, expounded Isai. 38:17 (*Surely it was for my welfare that I had great bitterness*) in respect of these people. For after the tyrants' persecution of the Church ceased, and she was herself endowed with many and great worldly goods, in truth many people, abusing this wealth, incited the Church to more bitterness by their enormous sins during this time of peace, than the bitterness that was felt during the persecution of the tyrants.

CHAPTER 2

<u>But there was a kinsman</u>. In this chapter, Ruth goes humbly and diligently into Boaz's field gleaning grain. The field signifies sacred Scripture, which is a field full of the best knowledge and sense, just like good fruit; and for this reason it is the field which the Lord blesses. Boaz, however, who is interpreted to mean "fortitude," signifies our Lord Jesus Christ, who is so much fortitude that *He sustains all things by his powerful words*, as Heb. 1:3 says. Truly the Lord himself is in this field, so that Deut. 33:2 says, *At his right, a fiery law*, which is contained in the Old and New Testaments. And it is well-named "fiery," because the fire of charity burns in the hearts of the faithful. However, the harvesters who belong to the man Boaz, that is, who belong to Christ, are the doctors and preachers. Ruth, humble and devout, signifies the devout and simple person who, by listening to sermons attentively, can derive things from them to inform her life and conscience; and the same is true for others, according to the means which suit them, by word and example. And concerning that, Br. Francis expounded 1 Sam. 2:5, *The barren woman has borne many children* etc. For he said the barren woman was the simple brother who does not have the office of preacher, through which sons (that is, the Church of God) are generated (1 Cor. 4:15, *In Christ Jesus I fathered you through the Gospel*). But such a simple brother, by leading an exemplary life, gave more to himself and to others than a verbose preacher; and the same must be said of other simple people who live exemplary lives. And this is well-signified by Ruth, who met with greater grace at the hands of Boaz than his harvesters did, because she became his wife. And so a simple person of exemplary life can meet with

greater grace at the hands of Christ, who is signified by Boaz, than his harvesters may, by whom (as was said) are signified preachers.

CHAPTER 3

When, however. Here Ruth's preparation for marriage to Boaz is dealt with; and this signifies the union of a devout person with Christ, which can be achieved by persevering in this present life. Therefore, Naomi, that is, the Church, says: Wash yourself with true and regular confession, because sins spring up frequently (1 John 1:8, *If we say that we have no sin, we deceive ourselves*).

And anoint yourself with an increase of grace, which is increased by sacramental confession.

Put on an increase of virtue, which is poured out with grace and is increased in its own increasing.

And go down. Through which it is signified that worthiness is covered by humility.

Take note of the place where he sleeps, that is, Boaz, through whom Christ is signified. However, the place where Christ sleeps with the sleep of the dead is the holy cross. To "take note of" this place is devoutly to consider Christ's passion.

And turn back. The feet are at the bottom, and so they signify Christ's humanity. Therefore, this uncovering signifies that suffering does not touch Christ except in His humanity, and so to uncover His feet means to hold firmly to the faith.[28]

Slip yourself underneath, for a connection of emotive compassion, and because such a person, who is joined to Christ through grace, desires to be joined to Him in glory. And so it says: Spread your blanket, by which celestial glory is signified (Isai. 61:3, *The mantle of praise instead of a faint spirit*). For those whose sins are washed away in the light of this present life are clothed by this covering. And so the Savior says Matt. 5:4, *Blessed are those who mourn, for they shall be comforted.*

Stay here tonight. The response of Christ to the person desiring Him is signified, through these words of Boaz, as has already been said; that is, by persevering in the night of the present age in a state of grace, until the future dawn in which all will be bright, and then your joining with me will be complete. And since as long as the devout person is in the present he profits by the gifts of God, therefore it adds "measures," by which the six gifts of the holy Spirit are signified, which are found in Isai. 11:2 (*The spirit of wisdom . . . and the fear of the Lord*). The Hebrew does not, in fact, have "the spirit of piety" (as I have said more fully in the literal exposition).

CHAPTER 4

Boaz went up. Here the joining in marriage of Ruth and Boaz is described, because the marriage was made when he who seemed the closer relative for the purposes of the contract with Ruth gave up his rights to her as the closer relation. And so Boaz took Ruth as his wife. The Church, which is illuminated by knowledge of the faith and of grace, is well-signified by "Ruth," which means "seeing." By the closer kinsman, John the Baptist can be understood. He was born before Christ and preached first and he was believed to be Christ, not only by the common people but even by distinguished people amongst the Jews. For this reason, they sent solemn messengers, that is priests and Levites, from the metropolitan city of Jerusalem, to ask him if he was Christ (and, in consequence, the bridegroom of the Church: John 1:19 *et seq.*). But John gave up the right which he was believed to have as the closer relative, saying, *I am not the Christ*, as we read in the same place. And likewise, chapter 3:29, where the same thing is said and more, *Whoever has the bride is the bridegroom*, where he shows that he is not the bridegroom of the Church but the best man; and so he shows clearly that the Church was kept for Christ just as a bride is, and Christ, who is understood through Boaz (as was said above), *took her as his wife.*

And through this, the royal genealogy is derived, coming from the progeny of Boaz and Ruth, when it says:

He was the father of Jesse etc. This signifies that they who are created from Christ and the Church in faith, and no others, will reign in heavenly glory. Which He who is blessed forever grants to us. Amen.

Translated from the Lyons, 1589, edition of *Biblia sacra, cum glossa ordinaria.*

Notes

1. The commentary appears to begin in mid-thought. The "third case" must refer to Ruth's place as the third (in appearance in the Bible) of the four women in Matthew's genealogy of Christ.

2. I.e., Peter Comestor.

3. In fact, he has six sons in Chronicles but seven in Samuel.

4. Jerome on 1 Chron. 4: *Quaestiones Hebraicae in . . . Paralipomenon, PL* 23:1373.

5. Nicholas consistently refers to quotations in Judges 11, which are now found in Judges 12, making it clear that his Bible was divided differently from ours. I have silently altered the reference, for the convenience of readers.

6. Rashi on Ruth, Breithaupt, p. 104.

7. Literally, "seed."

8. See Rashi on Ruth, Breithaupt, p. 107, who quotes "rabbini."

9. Cf. Targum (repeated in the Gloss Additions), which has a different group of four methods: Rashi on Ruth, Breithaupt, p. 108.

10. Rashi on Ruth, Breithaupt, p. 109.

11. Rashi on Ruth, Breithaupt, p. 109.

12. Matt. 1:17.

13. Rashi on Ruth, Breithaupt, p. 110.

14. Rashi on Ruth, Breithaupt, p. 110, note 7.

15. Ruth on Rashi, Breithaupt, p. 110, note 10.

16. Rashi on Ruth, Breithaupt, pp. 111–12.

17. Rashi on Ruth, Breithaupt, p. 112.

18. Rashi on Ruth, Breithaupt, p. 112.

19. Rashi on Ruth, Breithaupt, p. 113, note 9.

20. Rashi on Ruth, Breithaupt, p. 113.

21. Nicholas uses the word "reasonable" on more than one occasion to refer to Boaz. It may be that he wished to emphasize that Boaz's response to Naomi's (to later ears, improper) request, is simply in keeping with the Law.

22. This can only mean a relative of Maalon's own generation, that is, one of his cousins.

23. Rashi on Ruth, Breithaupt, p. 114, and notes 23 and 24.

24. I.e., that one of the six was the Messiah; Rashi on Ruth, Breithaupt, p. 115, n. 26.

25. Nicholas means that this text had a Messianic meaning for the Jews too.

26. Rashi on Ruth, Breithaupt, p. 116.

27. Deut. 23:3 continues: "Even to the tenth generation, none of their descendants shall be admitted to the assembly of the Lord." Nicholas (via Rashi) dismisses the possibility of the closer kinsman rejecting Ruth because he feared their children could never be counted amongst the children of God, for the Law here applied only to men: if their tribal positions had been reversed (Ruth an Israelite and the relative a Moabite) then the children would *not* have been admissible to God.

28. This seems most likely to mean "hold firmly to the faith" that Christ is both, and equally, human and divine; so that Jesus may suffer in his humanity, but Christ cannot suffer in his divinity. This orthodox insistence on the dual nature of Christ may be in response to the heresy of Adoptionism, a form of which was revived by Duns Scotus, a contemporary of Nicholas's and also a Franciscan. Scotus's attempts to produce an orthodox rendering of Adoptionism were unsuccessful.